ZANDER FISHING

A COMPLETE GUIDE

ZANDER FISHING
A COMPLETE GUIDE

MARK BARRETT

FOREWORD BY NEVILLE FICKLING

CONTRIBUTORS: JOHN CAHILL, DAVE MARRS,
LEIGH MCDONOUGH, DENIS MOULES,
DAVE PUGH AND IAN WEATHERALL

THE CROWOOD PRESS

First published in 2008 by
The Crowood Press Ltd
Ramsbury, Marlborough
Wiltshire SN8 2HR

www.crowood.com

British Library Cataloguing-in-Publication Data
A catalogue record for this book is available from the British Library.

ISBN 978 1 84797 018 3

Photographs pages 153, 154, 157 by kind permission of Colin Brett.

Line illustrations by Keith Field

Edited and typeset by Magenta Publishing Ltd (www.magentapublishing.com)

Printed and bound in India by Replika Press

CONTENTS

FOREWORD

Books on zander are quite rare, which is not surprising as the species is still largely confined to the south, midlands and east of England. This makes for limited interest in fishing for zander. Where that interest exists, though, there is an almost fanatical following. I think that it is good to be seriously involved in a sport that involves, in many cases, fishing against the odds in beautiful places at antisocial times.

This book might just increase that fanatical following. Mark has gathered together some interesting stories to inspire the reader, along with a no-nonsense approach to catching the fish. He dispels a few myths along the way, particularly the 'dropped run' problem, which is only really a problem if you are trying to catch tiny zander. He looks at all the waters he fishes in the Fens and gets guest contributions for those such as the Severn that he is not familiar with. Very little has been written about Severn zander so this book fills a big gap for those interested in what is probably our best water for big zander at the moment.

Having read the book I'm once again thinking of increasing my zander fishing effort. Whether I expand my efforts away from my local River Trent remains to be seen. Perhaps I'll be able to glean something from this book to help me. Whatever happens, I'll always have a soft spot for our wildest and perhaps least loved predator.

Neville Fickling

Neville Fickling with a good-sized zander.

ACKNOWLEDGEMENTS

This is my first ever book writing as the main author, and only the third book dedicated to the species. I sincerely hope that you will enjoy what you read. Though the book, on the whole, focuses more on the technical side of this great sport, I have also included some of the humour that the sport can produce and thereby provide the reader with a taste of what it is that drives so many anglers to try to land this most enigmatic of fish. In the pages that follow I recount some of the disasters that have befallen both my friends and myself, events that, when looked back upon, always give us cause for laughter. There to me is the essence of this great sport – the good times that we have to look back on and talk about, shared and recalled in the best of company – your mates. So it would be completely remiss of me to not offer my thanks to them for all the laughs, the triumphs and, of course, the disasters that have brought a whole lot of fun to all of us.

I would also like to thank those who have contributed to this book. Without them it would have been so much the poorer, and I thank them all for their time and effort in either putting pen to paper, or taking the time to let me into their thoughts about zander, and zander angling.

I also thank The Crowood Press for taking the chance on publishing this book, when in all probability they had never heard of me before. I hope that it swells their coffers, and of course my own! Also, James Holgate at Pike and Predators magazine has my deepest thanks, as it was he who actually saw something in my writing that many others missed. What exactly that was I don't know, but I am deeply indebted to James for giving me the opportunity to write regularly in a national magazine, especially one that I would read regardless of whether I was contributing or not.

Enjoying my fishing with friends will always be my first aim.

There are two other people that I should mention – my uncle and my father, both named Kevin, who first took me fishing as a child and who ignited a flame and a passion for fishing that I can see never being extinguished. I know that in my father's case there have been many times when he wishes that he hadn't done so, as another job was lost, or similar such disaster occurred because of too much time spent on the bank. However, without it there's no telling where life would have taken me, and I certainly wouldn't have had the many great memories from childhood that I will always carry with me. My parents have had to support me in certain periods of my life, and though it is possible they don't think that I have appreciated it, I always have, and I always will.

I would also like to thank Paul Garner from

Wychwood Tackle, whose company has in the past few years supplied me with equipment when I have managed to break, lose or damage my own in some way. I really do appreciate the company's support, and fully recommend their equipment and tackle to anyone.

Finally, a big thank you to all of you who have dipped into your pockets and spent your hard-earned money on this book. I hope that it will give you much pleasure and inspiration, and maybe add to your fund of knowledge about the zander. The picture on the previous page, my favourite of all my fishing photographs, may not be of a zander, but it sums up all that I enjoy about my fishing, and I am sure will touch a cord with all but the most confirmed loner.

May your string be pulled regularly!

Mark Barrett
September 2007

INTRODUCTION

Although the zander is hardly one of the most appealing species of fish in the UK, its popularity seems to be increasing year-on-year. Certainly, the number of anglers that I see on the banks of my home drains increases annually, and even the tackle trade has, in recent times, flirted with the idea of producing equipment specifically for zander fishermen.

Yet the aspiring zander angler is not well served by the angling press. The media as a whole, I think, still looks upon zander and zandering as a specialist aspect of angling, and as such, doesn't cater for the thirst for knowledge that characterizes most of the guys that I meet on the banks. There are little oases, though, if you really look. *Pike and Predators* magazine regularly runs articles on zander angling, as do *Coarse Angling Today* and *Coarse Fisherman* magazines. Even the weekly magazines will, from time to time, provide the zander with a bit of coverage and, most importantly, they discuss them in a less sensationalist way than in the past.

In terms of books, since Steve Younger's *Fenland Zander* (1996), there has only been *Zander*

The subject of the obsession.

(1979, new edition 1990) by Neville Fickling and Barrie Rickards to quench the thirst. Hopefully, the present book will bring the reader up to date with the latest in zander and zander angling. As with all aspects of angling, zander fishing moves on apace, and tactics and methods have to change and develop to keep track of these modern developments. To that end, this book includes information that the earlier writers would have struggled to cover, when the methods were very much in their infancy. Lure angling, and particularly the use of jigs, is a case in point. The recent explosion in lure angling for pike has seen many anglers who are prepared to be pioneers cross over to the zander world. Personally, I have yet to really crack this method and so have handed over the coverage of this aspect of zander angling to Dave Pugh, who really has got to grips with the methods required (*see* Chapter 9).

Likewise, the spread of zander throughout England has meant that the habitat from which zander are being caught has changed greatly. The likes of the Warwickshire Avon, the Severn and the Thames all now have good zander populations, and an increasing band of anglers that

seek those populations. Again I have gone over to friends for coverage of this aspect of zander angling (*see* Chapter 4), because although I have flirted with the species on the Avon I have not done enough fishing on these rivers to be classed as an expert on the fishing to be found there.

The zander has been found in England for over forty years, and though it is still seen by some people as an illegal interloper, in its spiritual home, the Fens, the zander is considered to be just another fish. That may seem like a bit of a bland description, but frankly it is all that those of us who lived through the infamous zander cull of the 1980s have ever hoped for. No more do you see the match angler knocking out zander and throwing them up the bank.

Zander is regarded as a game fish in some parts of Europe, and is often eaten. Accordingly, the main threat to zander stocks at present appears to be from either illegal immigrants or itinerant land workers, particularly from Eastern Europe. To that end, the zander angler needs to be observant as regards the activities of such, and to report what they see to the Environment Agency (EA). The EA are, alas, not capable of providing

Treating zander like this one is thankfully a thing of the past.

the manpower to prevent these activities and so yet again the angler needs to be the warden and keeper of the rivers.

Why Zander?

It would be remiss of me not to explain why it is that I choose to devote a large amount of my ever-decreasing spare time to the pursuit of zander, and what, I think, drives others onto the bank of river, drain or lake to do the same.

The first reason has to be that of testing of one's wits against a wild creature in spectacular scenery. A few readers may be thinking, 'Most zander angling takes place in the Fens – that's hardly scenic.' Well to a point I guess that they would be right; after all, the Fens have no mountains or hill ranges, little forestation and certainly no valleys, but here is a case in point of beauty being in the eye of the beholder. Whilst it would be true to say there is an absence of stunning geographi-cal features, this only enhances the view of the sky, for there is plenty of that in these flat lands. Only in the Fens can you get the staggering dawn and dusk landscapes that any good painter would give an ear or an eye for. A zander angler's dawn is a thing of beauty in its own right.

Aside from the sights and the places where we lock horns, there is much about zander angling that remains a mystery. Being as it is something of a minority sport, there is still only a relatively small band of anglers that chooses to pursue this species to any great extent. This has had the effect of making the learning process somewhat slower than for other species, such as the carp. Yet this learning process is another attraction of the sport. With the exception perhaps of the freshwater eel, I doubt that there is any other species in the country of which less is known, or regularly written about in the angling media. Even the catfish, another foreign invader, has more written about it; perhaps because their immense fighting abilities appeal more to the carp anglers.

A zander angler's dawn is a thing of beauty.

There can be few sights in angling to rival a big zander.

Despite the lack of in-depth knowledge of England's zander, still the number of anglers drawn to catch this species has increased steadily. For this air of mystery is now becoming an added bonus of zander fishing as the other species lose that veil of mystique that fires the angler from childhood. After all, if you can remember when you first began fishing, every venue held a monster, and a potential record was just one bite away. In this age of named fish, though making identification and, to a point, welfare easier, at a stroke the mystery that we enjoyed as youngsters has been removed. If you arrive on some waters these days, you can be provided with details of exactly what the swims are like, the stocking level, the top weight of the fish, and even their names and what they were last caught on. None of this is available to the zander angler.

Zander were officially only stocked once, in 1963 into the Great Ouse Relief Channel, from whence they spread throughout the Fens. Of course man being such as he is, the zander were given a helping hand to spread throughout the UK. This will probably continue until zander are widespread throughout England at least. However, for the greater part, these fish were seeded into river or drain systems when introduced, and so though man may have made the first move, nature had to finish the game, something she has done in style. This has resulted in zander being present in may waterways, yet no one knows to what extent, how big they grow, or how many there are. According to folklore, monsters swim in every venue, and a record can be just a run away.

Zander angling also has a mystique surrounding it for other reasons. As the fish itself is a lover of the dark, so the greater part of the zander angler's activity will be carried out after dark. To the outsider the zander angler must appear somewhat strange, in that he will spend days and nights in perfect solitude, often miles from anywhere, yet little will be seen of his presence, other than the bivvy from which he will only occasionally, vampire-like, emerge. The reality of the sport, of course, is known only to the zander angler for, unlike a lot of other branches of the sport, zander anglers on the whole are a pretty amiable bunch and there is far less of a web of secrecy that surrounds other branches of fishing. While it is fair to say that few zander anglers are going to automatically disclose their best swims or areas, the fact that zander, for the greater part, are mainly present in river or drain systems means that the venue (if not the area) can be revealed upon capture.

In the final analysis, the only person who can say why they go zander angling is the angler himself. The reason will almost certainly be different for each individual, though the points covered in this chapter will, I am sure, have all played their part to some degree. For me, zander angling is about all of the above, plus the chance to enjoy myself in the great outdoors with good friends and with the ever-present hope of coming face-to-face with one of England's most striking fish.

1 ZANDER TACKLE AND WHERE TO GO ZANDER FISHING

If you are going to do some zander fishing, you are going to need the equipment and clothing that will enable you not only to catch and land the fish, but also to withstand everything that the weather will throw at you. I am a sponsored angler, in as much as if there is any equipment that I want, I can usually get it free from Wychwood Tackle. However, all the equipment that is detailed here has been used extensively, either by me or my friends and, most importantly, we are all happy with it.

Of course, once you get into zander fishing you are likely to end up with many items of tackle and a very heavy rucksack into the bargain. The items I cover in this chapter are what I would call the basics, predominantly of course for bait fishing. It is up to you if you choose to add to these basic items. Lure fishing has its own growing band of followers, of which I am at the moment a rank beginner and happy to admit it. Therefore I have left it to Dave Pugh, who is much better qualified to give advice, to cover the tackle needed for this branch of the sport in his contribution to this book (*see* Chapter 9). The same applies for boats. I do use boats from time to time, for trolling the main rivers or on some lakes with limited access, particularly Roswell Pits. However, I don't use them very often and will therefore defer to those who use them more regularly, on the Severn and Warwickshire Avon in particular (*see* Chapter 4).

Rods

There seems to be a perception amongst some writers that because zander do not grow as big or, arguably, fight as hard as pike, soft rods more akin to barbel fishing will suffice. Well, to a point they will; however, you will be severely limiting the type of water that you can effectively fish. Waters such as the Great Ouse Relief Channel and Middle Level, where you are going to need at times to throw a bit of weight (lead and bait), are not going to be suitable for barbel equipment.

Personally I use rods of 2½ to 3lb test curve, as in my experience this type gives the best compromise between a playing tool and something that will punch 6oz of weight 50yd across a windswept drain. My rods are Grey's Prodigy dead bait and Wychwood Riot, in 3lb test curve. These rods

Good rods are a must for zandering.

have a progressive action and will cast a bait a good distance, but are not so stiff as to bounce out hooks from the zander's very bony mouth. Unfortunately, there are very few tailor-made rods dedicated to zander. Fox used to market the Zandermaster and the Predator Z. In my opinion the Zandermaster was just too soft, but the Predator Z was a more suitable tool. Dave Lumb Specialist Tackle used to market the Z1, and though I have never used or seen one, with Dave's reputation as a rod builder I am sure that these would be trustworthy tools.

In reality most rods could be pressed into service for zander, but fast-taper rods are unsuitable as these are just too 'tippy' in their action and you would lose a lot of zander.

Reels

To be honest, any reel that holds 200yd of 12 to 15lb line and has a good line lay will suffice for zander, as the very last thing any zander angler will want to be doing is fishing off a bait runner system, due to its inherent resistance. However, on occasion I do fish off the runner, in times of very heavy flow, or when trolling, but for the greater part of my fishing I will operate an open bail arm/drop off method of bite indication.

Notwithstanding this, the reels that I use for my zandering are Shimano bait runners, either the 10,000 or 6010GT versions. I use Shimano

Shimano reels are my first choice for all my fishing.

reels exclusively, not because of any commercial tie-up but simply because I have always found the line lay to be superb (which is very important when using open bail arms), and their build quality and reliability is unsurpassed.

Line

Line will always be a very personal choice, differing from angler to angler. My own preference is for any of the following – Berkley Big Game, Fox Barbuster, Fox Soft Steel, Wychwood Maximizer and Daiwa Sensor. Those represent a cross-section of budgets, with Daiwa Sensor being a good mid-range choice, and of equal quality to the more expensive lines listed.

One thing that is not acceptable as far as I am concerned is braid (other than for lure fishing, drifters or free-roving live baits). Zander fights invariably end with a lot of head-thrashing, right under the rod top, reminiscent of their cousin the perch. This is when you need the shock-absorbing properties of mono. I have tried braid, and very quickly binned it.

Bite Indication

As previously mentioned, I like to use a drop off type of bobbin for my zandering. These provide the best resistance-free set-up currently available. They do have limitations, particularly when the drains and rivers are running hard, but in this situation zander are far more tolerant to resistance and I will then normally fish direct to the bait runner, set to give at slightly more pull than the flow.

As for bite alarms, I favour front alarms as a lot of information on what is and is not a run can be deduced from a good front alarm, something not possible with rear bite alarms. I have yet to find anything on the market to touch the Delkim alarms. I have had mine for ten years and they have had very heavy use in that time, standing up to all that the Fen winds and rain can throw at them. Whichever alarm you choose, make sure

Good bite indication will help you to avoid deep-hooking zander.

that they have a track record of reliability, as a failing alarm is a recipe for a deep-hooked and possibly dead zander.

Hooks, Swivels and Traces

As with rods, a lot of nonsense is spoken about hooks and traces for zander. It is worthwhile remembering that wherever zander are to be found in the Fens, so are pike, and quite often they are big pike. It is totally irresponsible to use anything other than wire as a trace material. If you really are bothered about the trace affecting presentation use one of the range of soft strand wires available. My personal preference is for the Drennan range of wires, either the green super-

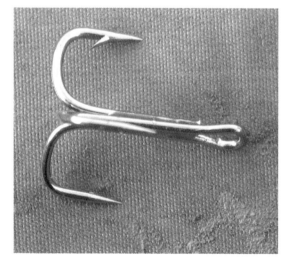

Wychwood Trebles are my first choice for bigger baits.

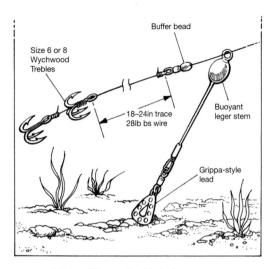

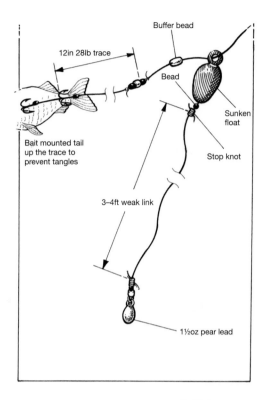

ABOVE: A legered live or dead bait rig.
RIGHT: A sunken float paternoster.

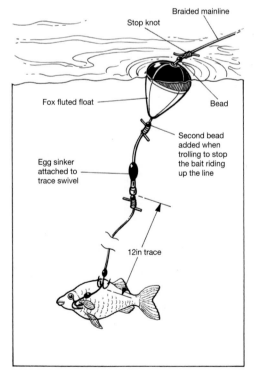

A free roving and float trolling rig.

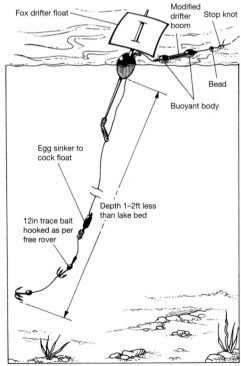

A drifter float.

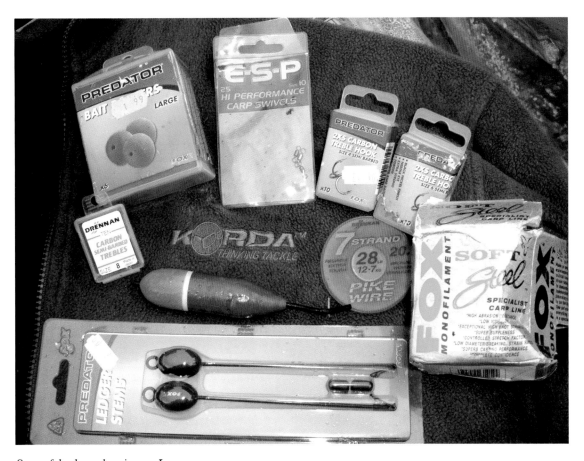

Some of the thermal equipment I use.

soft in 15 and 28lb, or the seven-strand in 28lb. The new 28lb seven-strand wire is very thin in diameter, and I don't think that this wire would spook fish at all.

As for hooks, well again it's the Drennan range for me, notably the carbon super-strong versions. I find these very sharp, fine but strong in diameter and able to achieve good penetration on the strike. I use these in size 6 or 8, and choose the semi-barbless. I see no point in dropping below this, as I don't use baits that are too small for a pair of size 8 trebles. Anything below an 8 will be very difficult to remove at night and will cause more problems than they solve. I also use Wychwood Trebles for bigger baits, as these match the Drennan hooks in many qualities, with just a touch more strength in the wire.

The Queenford retention, or giant barbel tube, which is by far the best retention method for zander.

Swivels are the simplest part of the rig, and I always use Korda. These have a nice matt finish, and are immensely strong.

Leads and Floats

Leads play a very important role in the effectiveness of the rigs that I use. Too light a lead, and the lead will drag on a take, resulting in increased resistance. To that end, when I need heavy leads I always use Korda gripper leads. These are flat in profile, with lugs all around, and don't move on a take. I usually carry a selection of these, from 4oz down to 1½ oz, for fishing over soft bottoms or weed.

I have to say that float fishing doesn't play much of a part in my zander fishing. On the rare occasions I use floats, I tend to favour small slimline floats fished through the middle, and preferably with no loading to them, or alternatively I use small bob-type floats. I do carry a few sunken floats, for sunken float paternostering. These are the smallest Fox versions, the ET foam-ball type or Drennan clear sub-floats.

In the Rucksack

I carry all my terminal equipment in a Flat Tackle box made by Wychwood, though Fox do a very similar one. In this will be spare swivels, hooks, superglue, bait poppers, trace wire, leads, bait tags, power gum, beads, leger stems, run rings, snap links, syringes, wire cutters, spare forceps and line grease. I carry my floats in a plastic Tupperware box, and my made-up traces in a rig bin.

Also in my rucksack will be a giant barbel tube and a Fox pike tube, used for retention. Alas, the giant barbel tube is no longer made; it is without question the best model I have seen, being based on the Queenford retention system designed by Phil Smith and Tony Miles, I believe.

I also carry two head torches and a hand torch (together with batteries for all of them), a radio to listen to the football and test matches, a Coleman stove for cooking on night sessions, weigh sling and Avon scales, live-bait tube, lightweight waterproofs, live-bait pump and batteries, tea bags, drifter floats and spare vanes, cameras inside a Fox camera bag, lightweight camera tripod, spare lighter and spare alarm in case of failure.

A walkie-talkie and a good torch are night-time essentials.

The other thing that I carry is a walkie-talkie. Some of the Fen drains that I fish, particularly the Middle Level, have very steep and potentially dangerous banks. I usually fish in company, but we do tend to spread out along the bank. The ability to call quickly for help could be a lifesaver. My handsets came from Argos and were £45 for three. Though the range is very much line-of-site, they are small enough to slip into a pocket and cheap enough not to worry about dropping in the water. Not something that you could say about most mobile phones!

Other Items

I have two carry-alls that I use for my zandering. If I am going on a long session, I use my 120 litre Nash pursuit rucksack. This is large enough to carry everything I need for a two- or three-day trip, including food. Most importantly, it is very comfortable and easy to use. It was bought second-hand, and is still going strong ten years later. For day-to-day use, I use a smaller 90 litre Trakker Holdall, as I find these easier and quicker to access when on the move. This will hold everything I need for a day or overnight session, and is comfortable to carry when on a two-mile hike to a distant drain hotspot.

For carrying the rods, bank sticks, landing net, storm rods, etc. to the bank I use a Nash Nomad 4 quiver. It fits on the shoulder well, and is more comfortable to carry than any other quiver I have used. It also fits my Groundhog neatly inside.

My landing net is a Wychwood 32in round net. I prefer the round nets as they are far easier to push through any weed in summer, and only require one hand to carry when a fish is landed, whereas triangular nets need to have both parts of the frame supported.

If you get serious about zander angling then you are going to need to do a fair amount of overnight fishing. This means that you are going to need shelter, something to sleep on, and warmth. I have tried a few bivvies in the past, but for the last three years I have been using a Nash Groundhog and I would recommend them without reservation. The Fens can cut up very rough, especially in regards to wind, as there are no hills to break it up. My Groundhog has stood up to the worst the English weather can produce, without leaking or becoming uprooted. It also has the advantage of being umbrella-based so can be used as an umbrella with extended wings, or with the zip-in front panel as an out-and-out bivvy. It is also very quick to put up and take down, which makes it very easy to move around. Three of my friends have also bought Groundhogs, having seen how well mine performs. They are not cheap; a full-system Groundhog will set you back £289, but if

it lasts as well as mine has it will be a sound investment.

A chair and a bed chair will also be needed – a chair for day sessions and a bed chair for overnighters. I use JRC Cocoon models for both of these. The chair is a Cocoon recliner, which can be laid right back for a sleep if the going is slow. The bed chair I used until very recently was a Cocoon three-leg. However, when an essential piece of plastic broke after eight years of sterling service I bought a Stealth three-leg version, also by JRC. I have to say that it is not a patch on the

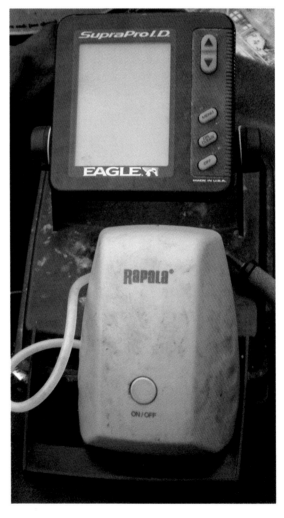

A bait pump is essential for keeping baits fresh. An echo sounder is equally important when boat fishing.

old Cocoon, and seems altogether more flimsy, so I shall be looking to repair the Cocoon as soon as possible.

If you are sleeping out you will need a sleeping bag. I use a Wychwood Extremis sleeping bag, which provides plenty of room for even my ample frame. In fact, most times I use it like a duvet as it is unbelievably warm, and I have slept out very comfortably in some cold nights.

Warm food and drink are vital in the colder weather. You can take a flask, but I prefer a Coleman Sportster stove or, for longer sessions, a double burner. These will boil a kettle in no time at all, though the Sportster stoves tend to have two settings – 'off' and 'blast furnace' – so cooking needs to be done with care. Stoves should always be handled with care, especially inside a bivvy, as bivvy fabric is flammable. Two additional items that I carry with me are an unhooking mat and

a bucket for transporting livelies, of course only from the swim where I have caught them.

On longer walks to distant swims, you are either going to have to load yourself up like a sherpa or, more likely, use a barrow. I have a Nash barrow, but I am not very satisfied with it as the wheels are too far forward. Whilst this makes the barrow stable whilst at rest, it also means that you take a large proportion of the weight on your arms, rather than the barrow taking it, which defeats the object somewhat. A normal garden barrow is sufficient, with the addition of a few holes drilled in the side to take bungee straps to stabilize the load.

This may seem like a huge amount of equipment to be carrying around, but with some careful planning it can easily be done, and when the result is a big zander in the torchlight, in my opinion it is definitely worth the effort.

When you add it all up, it amounts to a lot of equipment.

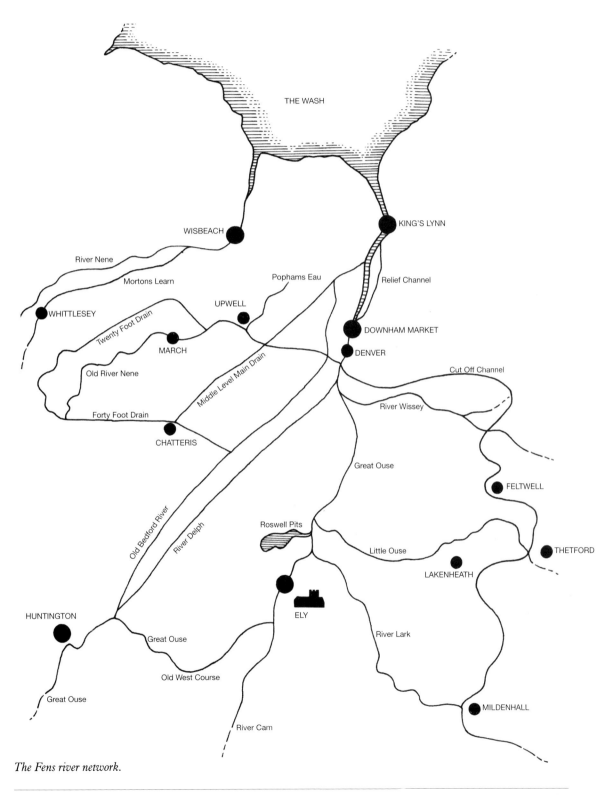

The Fens river network.

With the right tackle, zander can be brought to the net.

Where to go Zander Fishing

Although in the north of England there are very few bastions, the Midlands rivers and canals now have a good head. However, the zander is most common in the Fens. The entire major Fen drains and rivers contain zander. These include:

- Great Ouse and its tributaries;
- Relief Channel;
- Cut Off Channel;
- Middle Level Main Drain/Sixteen Foot Drain;
- Forty Foot Drain;
- Old Bedford/Delph;
- Little Ouse;
- Old Nene;
- Twenty Foot;
- Old West.

In addition, a few land drains will have isolated pockets of zander, as do the gravel pits at Fen Drayton and St Ives. There is a very good head of zander in Roswell Pits, which is connected to the Ouse.

Moving away from the Fens there are a lot of zander in the Warwickshire Avon and the lower River Severn, between Upton and Tewksbury, plus all the canals in the region. There are also a good number of zander in Coombe Abbey lakes. Also in the Midlands there are zander in the Trent, although only a smallish population at the time of writing. There are also some good zander in the Leicestershire Soar. Further south there are catchable numbers of zander in the River Thames and in the long-established Old Bury Hill Lakes in Surrey.

I am sure that there are many other smaller waters that have their zander populations but on the whole those waters mentioned offer the keen zander angler a realistic chance of their first zander encounter.

In later chapters I and other anglers will detail how to go about fishing the main zander waters. There are exceptions, in that the Trent and Thames are covered in little depth. The reason for this is simply that zander fishing on these rivers is still very much in its infancy. I am certain that in the coming years these rivers will have their own dedicated band of zander hunters, but at present there is not sufficient knowledge to write with expertise about these locations.

It seems logical, therefore, that the next chapter starts in the birthplace of English zander fishing, namely the Fens.

2 THE FENS: A GUIDE TO THE WATERS

When zander anglers think of the Fens it would be fair to say that most would think of the Fen drains. Built to drain the area and create what we now know as the Fens from the huge marsh that the area once was, the Fen drains criss-cross the area for many miles. Drains themselves vary greatly, from the large, windswept Relief Channel to the tiny land drains that you could almost jump across. All hold zander, though as you would expect some are better than others, having varying zander populations. But the Fens are not entirely about the drains. There are large areas of gravel pits and clay pits, and of course there is the Great Ouse system of rivers, all of which hold some very good zander.

Where it all began – the Relief Channel at Denver sluice – with ninety-seven of these (below).

Those ninety-seven soon grew up, into fish like this one from the Channel of 11lb 14oz.

One of the most pleasing things about living and fishing in the Fens is that you are never more than ten minutes away from a water that holds zander. In this chapter I will describe some of the better waters in which to catch zander, and explain how to go about fishing them.

The Great Ouse and its Tributaries

The best place to start is at the heart of Fenland, the Great Ouse River. The Great Ouse is in an upsurge at the moment, with the huge barbel, perch and chub caught in its upper reaches regu-

The junction of the Ouse and the Lark.

larly featuring in the media. However, for the zander angler the lower reaches are the most renowned for prolific zander angling. Flowing into or out of the Great Ouse are the Little Ouse, the Cam, the Old West, the Lark, the Hundred Foot Drain, the Relief Channel, the Cut Off Channel and many small unnamed land drains.

The Great Ouse itself is a wide, slow-moving, deep river in normal conditions. The main river is between 10 and 15ft deep, and is slightly brown in colour. However, in the winter after heavy rainfall the river quite often turns the colour of tea and can pull through at a frightening rate. I have been out on the river in a boat at this time of year, and can verify that an outboard engine is a must, as it would take all day to row a hundred yards against the current.

The Great Ouse's tributaries are generally shallower; in the case of the Little Ouse it is faster flowing and nowhere near as wide. Despite this, some of the tributaries are even better for zander fishing than the main river.

The Old West
I would recommend the Old West as the best river for the beginner to zander angling. This river joins the Great Ouse at Earith, just past Stretham. It has a huge head of zander of average size, but it

A typical Old West zander.

also has a few that are over 15lb. This river also fishes superbly for daytime zander, which can be something of an enigma on other drains or rivers. There are also some good pike in the river, although these are outnumbered by the zander.

It is worth looking out for deeper areas on this river, or areas where the fish can lie up out of the floods, as it is on average only about five to six feet deep. Marinas' boat-turning areas, or around the few bridges, are all good areas to try. The sport here can at times be truly spectacular, but thankfully, for some reason, this river gets overlooked in favour of its bigger cousin. To give you some idea of the sport you can have on the Old West, towards the end of 2006, in the space of two weekends, my fishing friends and I took fifty-two pike to 26lb and fourteen zander over 7lb to 8lb 8oz, with plenty of schoolies. On no occasion did we have less than ten pike or zander between us, and twice we each had more than ten.

The best tactics for fishing the Old West are leap-frogging live and dead coarse baits, either legered or paternostered, until you find the fish, and then sitting on the spot for a while. The fish in this river really tend to hold up together in numbers, and at certain times of the year there are areas where the fish hold up for several weeks ready to spawn. This is when the really big hits can be made.

The Cam

The Cam is almost the exact reverse of the Old West. It is crammed full of pike, with a much smaller head of zander. It is still a worthwhile water to fish, though, as year-on-year the zander population on the river is increasing both in numbers and in size. Doubles are more commonplace than they once were, and unusually the Cam is one of the venues in the Fens that throws up zander captures to sea dead baits, which is covered in Chapter 10 (page 102). The Cam is also the only place where I have seen a double caught

An Old West Marina double of 10lb 2oz.

on lures, this in over 80°F heat in the middle of the afternoon, and weighing 10lb 12oz. The better areas of the Cam, maybe not surprisingly, are closer to the confluence with the Great Ouse. As the Cam gets further away from the Great Ouse it gets shallower and tends to be a better pike and chub water.

The Little Ouse
The Little Ouse is somewhat of an enigma for zander anglers. That there are some big zander in the water is without question. I have seen fish of over 14lb, but they are thin on the ground and awkward to fish for, as the pike population of the water is very high. The Little Ouse is, on the whole, clear and with moderate pace in the lower reaches, and is quite fast in the upper reaches around Thetford. The river is, on the whole, quite shallow – around four to six feet deep. All baits work well, but live bait tends to produce a high percentage of small pike.

The Lark
The Lark is another shallow river of around four to seven feet on average, and is also quite clear apart from when the land drains pump water in during the winter, when it turns chocolate brown. There are plenty of pike present in the Lark but the average size is quite small, with a double being a good fish; however, a few surprises turn up every year. There are very few zander in the Lark, probably due to the clear, shallow water, but there is a large head of good perch. Perch of 2lb are quite common, and 4lb fish have been taken from certain areas. I spent some time on the Lark in 2007 in pursuit of these, and have found the best method is to float fish live baits. This should increase your chances of picking up a zander considerably, particularly schoolie-sized fish. However, in my experience this has never happened. I have my own theory as to why the river is a non-starter for zander fishing (*see* page 83), but one further reason for the river being so

The River Lark at Isleham.

poor is the fact that the confluence with the Great Ouse, or Lark Outfall as it is more commonly known, is one of the most popular zander swims on the river.

The Great Ouse

So to the Great Ouse itself, the main artery of the Fens. The lower reaches of the river, which are the best areas for the zander angler, have undergone a number of changes in the last few decades. Ten to fifteen years ago the Great Ouse had the reputation of being one of the finest winter roach venues in the country. I can well remember as a much younger fisherman sitting between anglers catching 30lb bags of roach, and pulling out schoolie zander and jack pike one after another.

Nowadays there are fewer roach in the river, though in recent seasons they have begun to make a recovery and are once again prolific, along with other species. Small skimmer bream are now prolific, with small ruffe and gudgeon also making a comeback, along with the biggest recovery story of them all, the bleak. The numbers of bleak on the river now are amazing. Five years ago it was rare to catch or even see one; now in the summer it's very difficult to get through them to the better-size fish, when bait catching.

Pike and zander populations in the Ouse have always been good, and this is still very much the case. The strange thing that I have always found with the Ouse is that you tend to have a pike day or a zander day. I have rarely had a day when I have caught roughly the same amount of both spe-

Glenn Gillett with a typical Ouse fish around the 9lb mark.

cies from the main part of the river; usually from day to day one species will prevail. However, the size of the pike and zander present in the Ouse seems to have dipped in the last ten years. An Ouse twenty-pounder is quite a rare beast these days. However, they are still around and if you really want to maximize your chances of a larger than average pike or zander you should get off the beaten track and try the more neglected areas of the river. Unfortunately, the main reasons why these areas are neglected is that access is mainly via a very long walk from the more popular areas. Nonetheless, the walk quite often pays off.

Good areas on the Ouse to try are around the bridges, drain confluences, marinas, bends and boat moorings. It also pays to study the match reports for the river, as the prey fish can become rather localized in the depths of winter. The town centre at Ely and around Littleport are both regularly good winter areas, but local advice is always the best, so try asking in the local tackle shops as to which pegs or areas are producing roach and bream.

The Ouse has pronounced shelves running along both banks, and pike and zander regularly patrol these. These are always the prime areas to place baits, but ignore the centre of the river at your peril. Although the middle can be very slow for pike, plenty of zander roam the centre of the river, and it is always worthwhile to place a bait there.

The standard tactics that I would use are to place a paternostered live bait along the near shelf, a dead bait to the far shelf and a legered live bait down the middle. As previously mentioned, the river tends to have one-species days and bait choice can also be like that, with some days deads outscoring lives and vice versa. Sea baits are always rather hit-and-miss on the Ouse, in my experience. Nine times out of ten I have found that coarse baits will be far more productive.

You may notice that I have made no mention of lure angling on the Great Ouse. Unfortunately I have found lure angling to be spectacularly useless. Although there are fish taken on lures every year, the shelves that are so successful for bait fishing make lure angling unproductive. To prevent your lure snagging up on the near shelf you have to reel the lure up in the water and over the heads of the fish that you are looking to catch. I am sure that the lure fanatics know of some lures that could be worked along the shelf; if they do then please let me know, as I would like to catch some fish from the Ouse on lures.

Ollie Newman returning a nine-pounder to the Ouse. The shallow shelves are clearly visible in this shot.

There is equal value to be had on the Ouse for both the mobile angler and the more static. The fish (perch excepted) tend to be very nomadic and runs can occur all day from one swim as new fish move through. Plenty of fish can also be taken leap-frogging,

The very bottom end of the Ouse at Denver.

but this can be difficult around the more popular areas. The same can also be said for boat fishing. I am only just beginning to troll the Ouse with live baits, but my first attempts have been encouraging. However, some of the better areas tend to be through Ely town centre and these can be difficult to troll as there are far too many other anglers around to allow long trolls before the rods have to be brought in.

The Ouse also has a habit of throwing up the odd surprise. Around the St Ives, Godmanchester and St Neots area there are some nice chub and every year a few mid-twenty pound catfish are starting to show up. Zander or carp anglers fishing live baits or fishmeal bollies at night mainly take these. I would not really consider these a realistic target, as they are few and far between at the moment, but maybe in the future the Ouse will have a healthy wels population, which would be of concern to the National Rivers Authority, but would be extremely exciting for the resident predator anglers. With the weights achieved in

mainland European river systems what size could an Ouse catfish obtain?

The Relief and Cut Off Channels

The Relief Channel has probably had more words written about it than any other Fen water, so there is little that I can add other than my own experiences of fishing there. This can be summed up in one word – hard. The Relief Channel is a big, imposing, hostile place and is not for the faint hearted. I personally could not recommend day fishing over night fishing, or vice versa, as both are as slow as each other. The tactics that I use on the Relief Channel are to fish a paternostered live bait on the near shelf, and on top of it if the drain is running off, a legered bait on the far shelf and a bait in the middle. To be honest, these are pretty standard Channel tactics, but until you actually get out and experience it for yourself it really is difficult to convey the feeling that you get for the place. I think it is best described as daunting in the extreme.

Looking down the Relief Channel from Denver.

Matthew Warren with a Channel eleven-pounder.

Despite all the negative points I have mentioned, there are several plus points. In recent years the small fish population of the Relief Channel has increased again. Several times recently I have stood on the stones at Denver and watched the fry and small fish topping all across it. Couple this with the low predator levels and you have the ideal conditions for growing on a really big zander.

In my experience the best time of year to fish the Relief Channel is in summer or autumn. It is primarily a flood defence measure for the Great Ouse River, and because of this in times of ever-decreasing high rainfall it is used to run off the excess water. Now this is certainly something to behold, as the water can drop by feet in 24 hours. However, it makes the fishing nigh on impossible, as the current will drag any baited rig into the margins in double-quick time. Having said that, zander anglers like my friend Dave Gaunt consider this to be the best time to fish the channel with jigs, letting the current bounce the jigs around the white water. In the summer, though, there are fewer occasions when the channel is run, and this means that the bait angler can fish far more comfortably. In fact, the fishing can on occasions be very good. Blanks are far less frequent than in the winter, although they are never too far away. If you don't visit the Relief Channel expecting to bag up, you may be pleasantly surprised. I have had three and four zander from the channel in the summer and I really like fishing the place. It is certainly one for the brave.

The baby brother of the Relief Channel is the Cut Off Channel. The Cut Off is not as wide or as deep as the Relief, and towards the end it narrows down to the size of a land drain. The main area that is of interest to the pike and zander angler is the area around the village of Hilgay, close to Downham Market. Here the channel is around twenty-five to thirty-five yards wide, about twelve to fifteen feet deep, and is clear and weedy in the summer. The area around Hilgay road bridge and Fordham bridge are the most popular, particularly in the winter when the channel gets packed with pleasure anglers fishing for roach, skimmers

A summer view of the Cut Off Channel.

and perch that move in during the colder months. Unfortunately, a lot of matches are held on this stretch in the winter for the same reason. King's Lynn Angling Club own the fishing rights on most of the Cut Off (as well as most of the major Fen drains), and to night fish for zander you will need a club book. Due to the amount of prime predator water that King's Lynn own, the £30 book is well worth the money.

So to the fishing itself. The Cut Off Channel is one of the few Fen waters to show little imbalance towards one species. There are equal numbers of both predators, but to get the best out of the zander prospects you need to fish at night. The lack of colour in the Cut Off makes daylight zander fishing patchy at best. Of course there are fish taken during the day, and one of the local US Air Force personnel used to catch plenty of zander in daylight, using rubber worm lures. However, the fact that these were all promptly placed in a cool box and taken back to base endeared him to the bailiffs and anglers no end.

Unlike most of the other drains mentioned, lure fishing is well worth a go on the Cut Off Channel. The water clarity and the close ledges make lures easy to work in, and they do take plenty of fish each winter. For all daylight and most night fishing I would strongly recommend the use of live baits. The baitfish shoals become so prolific on the main stretches of the channel in the winter that dead baits just do not gain the fishes' attention and are routinely ignored. In these situations I do tend to favour bigger baits. Roach and skimmers in the 4 to 8oz range are ideal for this, as they really do stand out from the crowd and grab the pike's or zander's attention. I know that some people hold the view that big baits are of little use for zander. In my own experience this is patently untrue; I have taken several good zander on roach baits of 8oz, and some much smaller ones as well. However, if you are really uncomfortable fishing using this method then keep using the baits that suit you.

My tactics on the Cut Off Channel, wherever possible, would be to leap-frog to cover as much area as possible. There seems to be large expanses of the channel that contain little in the way of predators and bait fish alike, so the more water you can cover the better will be your prospects. I would usually have two rods with legered lives on the far shelf of the channel, and one bait cast down the near shelf. Periodically I bring the far-shelf rods back a few feet at a time until they reach the near shelf, where they are left for a few

I tend to prefer bigger baits when fishing the Cut Off Channel in winter.

Cheryl Tomline with a Cut Off Channel double of 11lb.

minutes before I move on. The only time staying in one place works well in this location is if you can get tight under the bridges. However, if you wish to fish there you will need to be prepared to get up early as these are always the first swims to go. My own view is that it is far better to get off the beaten track a little and find some less pressurized fish.

For the greater part, the Cut Off Channel is one of the more comfortable drains to fish. The large flood banks and tree-lining help to keep most winds at bay, and the banks are for the most part quite flat and safe for night fishing. Also, the Cut Off Channel does not suffer very badly from heavy flows, except in really exceptional weather, and therefore it stays fishable when other drains are a turgid mess.

The Cut Off Channel has a good record for producing reasonable zander and pike, so what could you realistically expect to catch? Pike run to 20lb+, but they are few and far between, and in reality a low double is likely. Likewise with the zander. There are good fish taken every year, and with the amount of food present there remains the chance that an exceptional fish could be taken. However, the average size would be in the schoolie range (up to 5lb class). If you want to catch something bigger be prepared to put in the hours.

The Middle Level Main Drain/Sixteen Foot Drain

The Middle Level has quite rightly become established as one of the premier zander waters in the country, and in so doing has practically rewritten the top-fifty zander list in the process. But the area responsible for this phenomenon, the Main Drain, covers only a relatively small area of the

The bottom of the Middle Level with the famous pump at St Germains in the distance.

A Middle Level zander of exactly 10lb.

Middle Level system. There is plenty of other water, which, although maybe not as spectacular as the Main Drain itself, does still offer great sport with both pike and zander.

The other interesting thing about the Middle Level is that it has drains that change their name half-way down their length, which I think could only really happen in the Fens! The place to start, the Middle Level Main Drain, runs from St Germains to Three Holes. Here it changes its name to the Sixteen Foot Drain. It also noticeably changes its appearance and depths. Most of the Main Drain is steep-sided and reed-fringed, which does not change when it becomes the Sixteen Foot Drain. However, Main Drain is around thirty to forty yards wide, and is over sixteen feet deep in places; whereas in the area where it changes name it becomes narrower and shallower, with about ten to twelve feet being an absolute maximum, and eight feet more representative. Strangely, while the Main Drain can be pumped and run hard, the push seems to evaporate down the Sixteen Foot, which is rarely affected by strong flows.

On most of the Main Drain the fishing rights are run by King's Lynn Angling Club. They operate a day ticket system, and if you want to night fish the drain you must buy a season ticket,

which are available from most local tackle shops at a very reasonable £30 per season. The Sixteen Foot is run for most of its length by the Chatteris Working Men's Club.

Because of their differing characteristics, fishing methods can differ from one stretch to the other. As with most Fenland drains, both have pronounced shelves. In both of these drains they are tighter to the margins than elsewhere. The shelves are, again, major patrol routes for the resident predator population and as such are great places to put a bait. However, never ignore the centre of the drains, particularly for zander. My personal opinion is that some zander use the deeper areas of the middle of the drain as daylight refuges and quite regularly pack into these areas; this area therefore has the potential for larger than normal catches.

If I were fishing for zander in these areas I would concentrate on the Main Drain and fish mostly at night. However, although the Sixteen Foot Drain holds some good zander, it is also an excellent pike water and has in recent seasons produced a number of thirty-pounders, still very rare beasts on the Fens.

On the Main Drain I would use the following methods – free-roving live bait (daytime only), legered live bait (far and centre of the channel)

The mid section of the Middle Level at Neaps Bridge.

The Sixteen Foot Drain.

and paternostered live bait (on the near shelf). In the day I would also leapfrog up and down the drain to try and contact the zander in their laying up areas. The free rover I would cast to the far shelf and then try to work it around in an arc to the near shelf, and then work on beyond the rover and so on. At night I would drop the free rover and fish a legered live or dead bait well down the drain from my bivvy.

On the Sixteen Foot Drain I would dispense with the legers, and in their place I would use floats; my entire attack on this drain is based upon being mobile, and bite alarms and rod rests will just slow you down. Free rovers are once again a good idea on the Sixteen Foot, but I would cast them slightly further down the drain to start their arc as, due to the proximity of the

shelves to the margin and the steep-sided banks, you will probably spook anything sitting tight up to the margin in your very near vicinity.

Make the effort to get off the beaten track as much as is possible on both of these drains. Both have major access points that most anglers are drawn to, such as bridges or the famous Mulli-court Aqueduct. Sure, these areas can produce good catches, and I myself have caught some excellent zander by the aqueduct, but fish get wise, and move to more peaceful areas.

The Delph, Old Bedford and Counterwash

OK, are you sitting comfortably? Because you will need to have a clear head to understand the next 'Fenism'. The next drains that I am going to cover are the Delph, Old Bedford and Counterwash drains. Now the ridiculous thing about these two drains (no, that is not a misprint) is that the Delph runs under that name for part of its course, then becomes the Old Bedford; however, the Old Bedford is also the name of the drain that runs parallel with the Delph before becoming the Counterwash Drain. To cap it all, running parallel with both of these is the Hundred Foot Drain, or the New Bedford River, which is a drain, but is also tidal.

The Delph/Old Bedford is featuring increasingly regularly in my zander plans. The Delph is not a huge water; in most places it is only an underarm cast to the far bank. However, despite this it's a water with huge potential for an out-size zander, primarily because it is stuffed with prey fish and has a low head of zander. As we all know, this is conducive to producing the really big fish. What the upper potential for the water is, is hard to say, but I would not be surprised to see an 18lb+ fish come out in the future.

However, due to its low population the fishing on the Delph can be very, very hard. Blanks are more common than catching zander of any size. The large population of prey fish also serves to make the zander very well-fed, and is another reason why the fishing is far from easy, but it also means the average size of the fish is very good. In my experience the zander average around 7lb. I know of 15lb+ fish that have been taken from the drain in recent years, so it's definitely worth the effort.

The Delph – or Old Bedford.

The fishing itself is fairly straightforward, as the drain is only about ten yards wide until it reaches Welches Dam at Manea, where it starts to widen out slightly. However, nowhere along it would you really need to over-arm cast, and so straightforward float and leger tactics score highly. Free roving baits are difficult to use in the warmer months as the drain is very weedy and is usually lined on both sides by lilies, with dwarf lilies along the middle channel. These soon die off in the colder weather, but autumn and winter can bring along their own problems as the drain is very often run off and flooded with significant rainfall. The drain can stretch to 3 miles wide, as this is part of the Ouse washes, a world-renowned area for over-wintering migrant wildfowl. This can make fishing nigh on impossible. I know that some people have persevered and caught zander in these conditions, but personally I would rather look elsewhere.

The Counterwash/Old Bedford River is very different to the Old Bedford in that it is only ever lightly run off, and is very shallow and weedy for most of its length. In all honesty it is not much of a zander water until it becomes the Old Bedford at Welches Dam (where the Old Bedford of lower becomes the Delph), and even then the population is very low, but on occasion can be very high. I don't have a great deal of experience in fishing for zander here, as I find night fishing for them quite dull on very small waters like this. I have pike-fished it a lot, and it gave me my first ever 20lb pike, but as far as zander goes it's there for those anglers wanting to pioneer and is not really my cup of tea.

Separated from the last two drains by just a few yards is the New Bedford River. As previously mentioned, the river is tidal and can rise and fall an appreciable level, as well as flowing in different directions. Because it is fast-flowing and runs through the rich Fen soil, the New Bedford is always coloured and also very liable to flood,

An 11lb 11oz Delph zander.

A 9lb Old Nene zander taken in daylight.

although not to the extent of the Old Bedford. Due to this colour the New Bedford has quite a healthy population of zander and is possibly one of the most underrated of the Fen rivers. I know of at least one fourteen-pounder that came from the river and have seen photos of some very big zander taken from the river in the 1980s. The river is probably overlooked due to the fact that it is without question the most uninspiring stretch of water that you are ever likely to see. However, it is currently heaving with small fish, including gudgeon, dace, chublets and bleak, all of which are ideal prey fish for zander. Unfortunately the fast current does greatly restrict the use of anything other than legered baits. I have always found that live baits out-fish dead baits on this water.

Significant Others

Of course there are plenty of other waters in the Fens that hold zander in varying degrees. The Old Nene is another river that has a reasonable head of zander in it, as has the Great Raveley Drain that links into it. They are a realistic proposition to go out and target, and interestingly they are good locations in which to find daytime feeders.

The Twenty Foot Drain also holds a consider-

The fish of Fenland dreams. Glenn Gillett with a Middle Level 15lb 5oz fish.

able number of zander that can be caught quite readily in daylight, and it has higher than average sea bait captures, possibly because of the amount of piking that takes place here. Pophams Eau is another overlooked water. As it runs into the Sixteen Foot Drain at Three Holes there is theoretically no reason why any zander could not go up that drain rather than the Sixteen Foot or Middle Level drains. However, it just doesn't seem to be as productive, or at least it never has been for my friends and me. There have been some good zander out of the drain, and I am sure there will be more again. If you are looking for somewhere really quiet then I would strongly

recommend the place, as I rarely see anyone on there these days.

The list of waters could go on and on, really. As zander have spread throughout the Fens they have populated most waters, some more than others, but invariably there will be a small zander population in even the tiniest of land drains. They may not be a realistic target species, but they can make a nice surprise when piking. However, there is certainly scope in a lot of waters for the more pioneering zander angler because, as with most fish species, those first few interlopers really can turn into the giants that we all seek.

3 FISHING THE FENS

I imagine that just about every article or book ever written about the Fen drains will at some stage mention how featureless and boring they are. Having fished on Fenland drains and rivers for many years now I have to say that this is, in my opinion, quite misguided. However, you really have to know what you are looking for, as the features and fish will not all be immediately noticeable.

Shelves and Margins

Let's start with rivers. Most Fenland rivers will have a near and far bank shelf. On all rivers this is a huge producing feature, on some it is the main one; however, where there are shelves there will also be shallow areas on top. These can be features in themselves, and not just as you would expect in the warmer months. On the Little Ouse

The author with a 12lb zander taken from the far margin.

in particular there are some stretches that have large shallow margins before the shelf. I have regularly taken fish from on top of these shelves, both near and far. So why should a zander come up into such very shallow, cold water? I believe this is for two reasons. First, they are scavenging for anglers' discarded baits. Most anglers that I have seen just flick unwanted bait into the margins, and the zander are wise to this source of food, as early in the morning and at last light the zander will regularly patrol these areas looking for a free meal. Second, they are looking for fry. In most waters the fry will use these shallow areas as a relief from periods of strong flow. Unsurprisingly, perch in particular which will come right into the shallows at all times of year to hunt amongst the cabbages that proliferate on most Fen drains.

Before I leave the shelves it is worth mentioning the part that aquatic plants play in their attractiveness. A lot of drains will have quite large rush beds, and most also have lilies and cabbages. As well as being attractive hunting areas for perch, cabbages harbour pike as well, although this usually only occurs in the warmer months or in periods of high water levels. As far as zander are concerned, I believe plant life plays a smaller part in where they are found. I have known zander to come from under lilies in high summer, but rarely have I found them as productive in the winter, in part due to the fact that the lily tends to grow in shallow water, which is obviously very cold in the winter, and even in the floods I have not found lilies to harbour zander in any great numbers. This is probably because zander cope surprisingly well with floodwater and heavy flows.

Some Dutch anglers I have come across on the Internet believe the zander is capable of dealing with heavy flows, as their shape allows them to hug the bottom of the river and iron themselves down, similar to the way barbel deal with the flow. Whether this is true or not I cannot say for certain, but it is something to bear in mind. Reed beds certainly hold and attract all predators, because the prey fish that will take

Zander cope well with strong flows and floodwater.

Rick Warren with an Ouse biggie caught from the bottom of the shelf.

A 12lb Ouse zander taken from a series of bends.

sanctuary within them. For pike and perch I would fish tight to the reeds, but for zander I would drop to the bottom of the shelf in front of the reeds, as the zander prefer to hang off in the deeper water and attack up when the light fails and the prey fish feel safer to leave the protective cover.

Cattle Drinks

One of the best features I have found on all drains is the cattle drink, by which I mean any significant cut back and shallowing up of the bank. In the past these were far more prevalent than they are today, and have become scarcer as the River Authority has built up the banks, and the drinks become unusable. This is a crying shame because they can be invaluable in the winter floods as they create great slack water areas, and therefore refuges for that year's fry.

Having said that, stretches of the Ouse, Old

West, Little Ouse and parts of the Old Bedford/ Delph still have a number of them. There are lots on the Old West in particular, as the riverbanks are regularly used as pasture land. The thing to ascertain with either the cattle drinks or cut backs is their depth. Most proper cattle drinks will be very shallow, and rarely do the predators hold in them but they will be hanging around the general area.

Cut backs in the bank, however, quite often tend to be deeper, perhaps only a foot or so shallower than the river proper, and in these cases pike in particular will be holed up in them and are normally reluctant to leave them. I can think of no better example of this than on one of the very rare occasions that I have fished a pike match. The match was held on the Old Bedford and the draw for the pegs took place on top of the riverbank outside a pub. Opposite where the draw was taking place was a very fishy looking cut back, and almost all the anglers were saying how they liked the look of the swim but would not really want it, as 60 or 70 anglers were standing on top of the bank at that moment in time.

I bet you can see what's coming next, and I won't disappoint you. The angler who drew that peg cast straight out into the cut back and, hey presto, one 24lb pike later he won the match!

Side Drains

Side drains tend to differ greatly, and their attractiveness is influenced by a variety of factors. Many side drains in the Fens are a direct result of the drainage system, and as such come complete with attendant pump house. Now these pumped drains can really move some water in the wintertime, and they create depressions in the main

drains where the pumped water hits the riverbed. The depressions are usually slight, rarely more than a foot or two. However, they can really hold fish, more so in the summer than the winter as the discharged water from the side drain is invariably very coloured and complete with all the normal rubbish that you would expect.

Few predators find sitting very close to this water comfortable. As usual, though, there are exceptions. On the Lark, which I fish regularly for perch, there is a pump pool where the best spots are right around where the pump water comes out. This is because the pool itself is quite large, and is a great refuge for the fry when the main river flows through hard. In fact it sees large numbers of small fish through from the first floods to the end of the season. Obviously this is what draws in

Side drains can be potential hotspots.

the perch, and a few pike too. But it will still hold fish even when it is pumped regularly. There are two reasons for this. First, there is refuge within a refuge. Much like in a weir pool the fish head up under where the water is pumped and to the side of the pumps where the water is barely moving. Second, once the initial floods have taken place the pump switches over to a level monitoring or timed pumping. What that means in reality is that the pump will switch on once or twice a day to keep the water low around the fields, but will stop after a short period of time, and fish can be caught again very quickly after this pumping has stopped. Of course, you need to have all that information to hand before it can be ascertained as to whether it will hold fish or not. The alternative is just trial and error.

Before I leave this type of drain it is worth mentioning the other side of the pump. On a lot of these small land drains the pump pool can be the only wide part of the drain, but the fish that these pools holds can be quite staggering. I have regularly caught pike from these tiny drain pools and one of my regular fishing partners, Ollie Newman, has had two 28lb pike from such waters, so they are always worth a go.

Alongside the pumped drains there are normal drains, which have little in the way of flow. The effect of these on the main carrier is an area of shallow water on top of the shelves where the silt, etc., has been deposited from the side drain. Because of their shallowness I have rarely found these areas to be very good. However, in some cases they do result in a bottle-necking of the river where the additional build-up from the deposits makes the shelves wider. They can also hold fish when the river is flooded, especially within the drain itself.

Twists and Turns

Some of the best features of Fen drains and rivers are their bends, twists and kinks. If the river twists and turns a couple of times or more then that is even better. Obviously some of the drains have fewer bends than others but few drains, if any, have no bends.

I cannot stress too strongly how much I rate these as predator holding areas. Whether it is the disruption of the flow that harbours the predators, or prey fish that in turn attracts them, I cannot say with any certainty. All I can say is that the amount of good catches I have taken from bends is legion. In fact just about every one of my favourite stretches of drain or river has a bend or an 's' bend in it somewhere.

Bends are reliable holding features.

Dredgers and weed cutters can alter the complexion of a drain.

I would put bends into a category of their own, in that they are bank-side rather than sub-surface, but the thing to remember is that what you see on the surface will nearly always have some bearing under water, particularly on drains where features are in shorter supply. Extremely subtle things can make the world of difference to a swim and make it stand out from other parts of the same drain. For example, one drain that I fish regularly is, for long stretches, the arche-typal Fen drain in that it is straight, although quite weedy. Now I can honestly say that I have rarely found true hotspots on the drains but I did on here. The defining point? A single bush that hung slightly over the water, and not a very big bush, either. I had my first-ever 20lb pike from that swim, along with stacks of doubles. The only

zander that I ever saw from that particular drain also came from that swim, along with a 3lb+ eel one day on a smelt. Boy was I pleased with that! But the point is that one change to the scenery attracted those fish. There was nothing else to that swim; believe me, I tried to find it. But this can regularly be the case, with bank-side trees, bushes, etc. making a feature underwater.

If the drain that you choose to fish is regu-larly dredged I would look for something on the bank that would impede the dredger's progress, assuming it is dredged from the bank. Most of the bigger drains are dredged from the river, but smaller drains still use the tracked dredgers. Ex-amples of such obstructions are narrow gates by the waterside, power lines, trees, etc. All these mean that the dredger will miss an area, leaving it shallower. Pike, zander and perch love these areas. I can remember one session where two friends and I hopped along the Old Bedford on an increasingly rare day when the river had dropped back after a flood. Runs came thick and fast, but although we had taken over thirty pike they were all jacks, until by luck it was my turn to hop and I hopped by a farm gate. There followed the only three doubles that we had all day, all taken fishing around the drop-off. On this particular day the pike got there first, but you could very easily substitute zander on another day.

Transient Spots

The final feature that I would like to cover is by nature a transient one – wherever the prey fish are concentrated. Most of our predator fishing is done in the colder months. Prey fish will at this time tend to shoal up, and where they were once scattered along the course of the drain there are now large areas devoid of prey fish.

The obvious way to find the prey fish is to read the match reports, speak to other anglers, and so on. Also, some of the features mentioned earlier will hold prey fish concentrations. Any stretch of river/drain that runs through a populated area is another likely spot. I cannot recall anyone ever giving a scientific reason for this migration but it certainly does take place. On the Ouse, Ely town centre comes alive in the winter for predator and prey alike, as does March town centre for roach on the Old River Nene. Of course, these are always worth bearing in mind if you can put up with all the attendant problems that come with

Town centre stretches are good transient spots, as they tend to harbour great numbers of prey fish in the winter.

town centre stretches and I have to say unless I am bait catching I avoid them like the plague; they are just too stressful.

One last thing to look for is a bream shoal. If I have read in the press that bream are consistently showing in an area then I will be down there like a shot. Zander swarm madly around bream shoals. Why exactly they do so is a matter of conjecture, and is discussed further on page 78, but my belief is that the cloudy water caused by the bream feeding gives the zander the chance to sneak up on the smaller members of the shoal or any small fish also stimulated to feed. The zanders' superior eyesight will then enable them to cause carnage. It's only a theory, but so many zander anglers subscribe to it that there must be something in it.

I will regularly drive the course of a chosen drain until I find a pleasure angler who has been or is catching bream, and it nearly always works. It did so in style for me on the Ouse in 2007. I had driven the course of the river and no one was catching much. However, I came across a chap who had caught four decent bream and was packing up, so I jumped in behind him. In the next six hours I caught zander of 6lb, 7lb 10oz, 8lb 11oz, 9lb 9oz, and a clonker of 14lb 2oz. The next night my brother Paul and I returned to the same spot; I took fish of 7lb 4oz and 9lb 10oz, and Paul took the honours with fish of 6lb, 8lb 10lb 10oz and 11lb 7oz. I also lost a good double right at the net, and to complete the story, just as the floods started a couple of days later a friend

Bridges alone won't turn a poor zander area into a good one.

of mine took a fish of 10lb 11oz, so you could say that it was a reasonable swim.

Bridges

One final feature that is often quoted in relation to zander fishing, and in fact all Fen predator fishing, is bridges. I have very mixed feelings on the reliability and viability of bridges as zander-holding features. I am sure that at times there are zander close by, and under bridges, and can think of many places on the Fens where bridges are good spots. However, I can think of far, far more where they are of no use at all. My view is that bridges are far more likely to draw in prey fish than predators. Of course, by doing so they do naturally bring predators to them, but I sincerely doubt that those zander would be there otherwise, at least as a regular comfort zone to retreat to.

It would be an unwise angler who wrote off bridges as potential zander swims completely, however, because, for whatever reason, there may from time to time be some zander in the vicinity. Just bear in mind that a bridge alone will not turn a poor zander area into a good one.

Find the features, find the zander.

4 THE WARWICKSHIRE AVON, THE WEST MIDLANDS CANALS AND THE RIVER SEVERN

John Cahill

In some ways, given the contrasting type of waters in the West Midlands compared to the Fens, this subject is a book within a book. Consequently I asked my good friend John Cahill to provide an insight into the West Midlands. John is a company director and family man who now utilizes all available time on the Midlands waters, having fished across the British Isles over the last three decades. He is a former Pike Anglers Club of Great Britain regional organizer and liaison officer, and is the current membership secretary for the club. In addition, John is also a consultant to the Fishing Pool Ltd.

Introduction

When Mark asked me to write on the subject of zander my immediate thought was, who can I get to do it instead as my zander experience is only a new-found fascination. However, whilst I am only on my fifth season devoting time in pursuit of zander, when I gave the request some thought I realized that I do know the rivers well, and, more importantly, I know a fair number of anglers who have had success catching zander.

At times in recent years it has felt like there were only a handful of anglers who regularly

John Cahill with a nice zander, and a truly stunning backdrop.

devote time to catching large zander. I was on the river mainly at weekends, but made occasional midweek trips too. This chapter owes a lot to the input of anglers I know and see regularly on the waters.

The Warwickshire Avon

The Warwickshire Avon is a very picturesque river running from Warwick to Tewkesbury, with the pleasant towns of Stratford, Evesham and Pershore along the way. Navigable for 40 miles from Stratford to Tewkesbury, it has many attractive Warwickshire villages on its bank-side, with equally appealing pubs on a long, hot summers day.

Navigation was opened in the seventeenth century, with ongoing voluntary restoration now being undertaken by members of two charitable trusts, whose activities are funded by licence fees and donations. The Lower Avon Navigation Trust is responsible for the stretch from Evesham downstream to Tewkesbury, and the Upper Avon Navigation Trust looks after the stretch from Evesham upstream to Stratford, although their authority is as far as Warwick only, as the latter part is not navigable. The Trusts regularly check that the appropriate licence is held on their parts of the river, especially on manned locks. So if you do intend to launch a boat please ensure you hold the appropriate documentation and insurance. The navigable section of the river is very popular with leisure boaters during the summer months. It also has seventeen locks, some of which are manned.

Kill, Kill, Kill

Over recent years electro fishing has taken place on the river and a 'kill all zander' mentality exists amongst some of the pleasure/match fraternity. This is despite a 2002 Environment Agency (EA) survey revealing that a Warwickshire Avon tributary had the UK's highest fish population density at 11kg per 100 square metres. Declining match results are often blamed on predators, but having fished the river since the 1970s and witnessed significant change I take a different view. Water

quality is nearly gin clear at certain times and, given the EA results, I believe the silver fish have changed their feeding habits from the middle of the day, which suits the pleasure/match angler, to dawn and dusk feeding times. If anyone doubts this, they should visit the river regularly in the early morning or late evening in the summer as I do, and witness the amount of surface activity. If that doesn't convince you then get on a boat with an echo sounder; parts of the river are 'black' with fish.

Thankfully electro netting appears to have ceased for now, and if the zander are given time to find a balance then all angling disciplines can enjoy their respective branch of the sport. Credit must also go to Matt Hayes and Mick Brown, who have argued the zander's case both on TV and in print in recent years.

Distribution and Methods

Zander are spread throughout the Stratford to Tewkesbury length and can turn up on any stretch. Finding specific swims or lies on those stretches is the key. When not in flood the river has a slow-moving pace and I have had fish on all the usual methods, i.e. live baits, dead baits and lures. Bait fishing rigs are illustrated on page 16, but we use all of the following methods for either live or dead baits – paternoster, pop-up legered, legered with bait on the deck, trotted baits under a float. Provided you get your indication methods right all of these approaches can be used on bank or boat. One method seldom used is the classic dead bait sink and draw. Braid was made for this and the rig need consist of no more than braid to a trace with sufficient weight to get the bait to the bottom in the flow. I tend to use a very small arsley bomb attached to the trace swivel – there is no need for fancy rigs from Europe, when you have sink and draw in your armoury.

For the visiting angler the Avon has a host of day ticket stretches that can be found via an Internet search, or from clubs such as the Birmingham Anglers Association and the Stratford Anglers Association. Now I could be specific and detail precise locations and even swims, but you knew I wouldn't do that didn't you! All I would

A nice Avon zander.

say is, do a bit of research, think about the river and what's under the surface when you get there, and have fun. Remember, it fishes hard for the venue regulars at times.

Bank or Boat?
I fish from both the bank and a boat, but enjoy using a boat on most visits. However, I would argue that neither one has an advantage over the other, with the exception of lure fishing. Yes, you can catch zander on lures from the bank, but the frustration of snags and lost lures may well drive you crazy. On the boat you will also hit snags, but with a good lure retriever will get your equipment back nine times out of ten.

One big advantage of boat fishing is the ability to 'map' stretches using an echo sounder, and you can also get a feel for what the bottom consists of. On one of his Sky TV programmes Matt Hayes mentioned zander in proximity to mussel beds; I have also found that. I know zander like flow over them, and if mussels do too that would explain the connection. Keep things simple, though – if you find decent depth, flow and the occasional mussel/gravel bottom, give it a go. Depth changes and gullies can also reveal fish. It is certainly interesting trying to understand zander; my friends and I have a few radical theories of our own that we plan to investigate.

Potential

Double-figure zander are a realistic prospect from the river, although they are by no means easy to catch. In recent years fish in the 15, 16 and 17lb class have been caught, and a 17lb 2oz lure-caught river record was reported by Simon Pocock in March 2005. Larger fish have also been claimed.

Targeting large fish is not easy, and certainly some of the big fish captures have had an element of luck to them, sometimes falling to pike anglers. Time spent on the river in the right locations will assist, but equally the visiting angler could strike lucky and land a large fish. However, the odds are stacked in favour of the local angler who can fish when conditions are right.

One interesting aspect of the Avon is that it has been a relatively poor 'large pike' river, with double-figure fish rare. Yet zander, when left to

self-regulate and find a balance, appear to be getting bigger. Perhaps the Warwickshire Avon will be the 'dark horse' of the zander specimen world in the coming years.

The 2005/2006 Season

While I was developing my knowledge of zander I had identified a stretch of the river I suspected might hold a better stamp of fish. It was not until the Autumn of 2005 that I tried it with Steve Tighe and from my boat I caught fish of 10lb 4oz, 10lb 2oz, 9lb 8oz, 8lb 10oz, 8lb 8oz, 8lb 6oz and 7lb 8oz, all in the space of two hours, and Steve had a personal best of 8lb 8oz as well. Numerous smaller fish were not weighed. A concentration of this size of fish during the middle of the day is a very rare occurrence; I therefore went back four days later and had a 9lb 8oz and a 7lb 6oz

John displays a fine zander in the rain.

53

too. After that the river flooded and shifted the feature they were holding to. The swim has since produced nothing.

The West Midlands Canals

The Midlands have an extensive canal network, and zander have been found in, amongst others, the Coventry, Oxford, Grand Union, Stratford upon Avon and Ashby canals. It is probably not appropriate for me to provide more precise information about the location of zander in the canals of the West Midlands because, unfortunately, British Waterways have been in the habit of electro netting and killing all zander. Although this practice has stopped in places I have no wish to aid and encourage it in any way. In my opinion, British Waterways should leave zander alone to see if a balance can be found, as electro-netting

will not rid the canals of zander and in many ways is a waste of resources. I do not think that zander should be used as the scapegoat for diminishing angler numbers, as these anglers are all to be found on purpose-built carp waters.

The dilemma for the zander angler fishing the West Midlands canals is that most of the network sees a very shallow depth, often only two to three feet all the way along, with little variation. This provides the prey fish with virtually no cover from the all-seeing zander, and consequently zander numbers do not appear to find the balance I talked about on the rivers, where schoolies dominate. That said, fish into double figures have been caught, such as one by a good friend of mine, 'Mad Mick' Bowen, a well-known character from Redditch. Nonetheless, as can be the way with the canals, the venue where Mick caught the fish from was drained and netted the week after the capture.

The West Midlands canals have proved to be a great home for zander, being very similar in character to drains like this one.

So where do you start searching for canal zander? The only way I have done it is to get out there, walk the canals and fish. I use only lures, which will not be everyone's choice, and I only fish the canals in the close season, but apart from my own friends I have never seen another zander angler in all my time on these waters. To see another fisherman is rare, as the pleasure/match anglers have moved to the easy carp puddles. So, if you want a challenge and want to fish virtually unfished waters then the Midlands canals may be for you.

The River Severn

The River Severn is the longest river in Britain, at about 350 miles long. It rises in the Cambrian Mountains in Wales, and has three distinct stages before it reaches the Bristol Channel:

Source to Shrewsbury	Upper Severn
Shrewsbury to Worcester	Middle Severn
Worcester to Gloucester	Lower Severn

It is the lower river that is of particular interest to the zander angler.

The lower Severn is a wide and deep river that in normal flow has an even but powerful current. Often referred to as a canal in this area due to its wide and seemingly featureless straights, it has depths of up to 20 to 22ft in places. In conversation with locals you may well hear the words 'above' and 'below', which refers to above or below Tewkesbury weir. These two sections of the Severn differ, with 'above' having an average depth of about fourteen feet and 'below' 8 to 10ft. Below the weir the river is wider and more coloured due to tidal influence. Whilst the water is neither saline nor brackish, the tide is something you need to be aware of both from bank and boat.

The upper Severn.

Ken Lancett with a 12lb 10oz Severn zander.

Weirs below Tewkesbury stop tides below a height of 8m. The only effect this will have on the section below Tewkesbury is to slow the river flow down. Tides above the 8m mark can cause the river to come to a standstill, before flowing in the opposite direction, with possible rises in the water level of 2 to 4ft. Extreme conditions can result in a rise that will cause the water to top Tewkesbury weir, which came as a considerable surprise to two of my friends some years ago as they boat fished the weir at anchor and at night. On the occasions when the Tewkesbury weir is flattened out, the tidal effect can be felt on the Tewkesbury to Worcester stretch. Boat fishing the weir has recently been banned by local clubs. Whether this continues, and a historic venue is lost to pike and zander anglers, remains to be seen.

Floods

The scourge of the river-boat angler, floods can cause the Severn to rise very quickly, and it can be slow to fall. Dramatic TV reports show the most severe cases involving the flooding of houses and farmland, but it is not a new phenomenon – even the Romans built flood defences on the river.

During the autumn/winter season the river can be unfishable from the boat for most of the prime part of the season. Couple this with a three-month close season and a busy summer for recreational craft then you can have a frustrating time on the Severn. If you are not local to Worcestershire or Gloucestershire, the water-level hotline is a crucial source of information. I fish the river regularly, but in the early days I often wasted petrol on a 100-mile round-trip by not checking the trends on the river. The 2004/05 season proved particularly difficult as it seemed that every weekend the river, whilst not in flood,

Ken with a 10lb 4oz zander caught from the bank in the floods.

was not quite right. The 2005/06 season saw a cold and dry winter, and again conditions were far from ideal.

For those not used to big rivers my advice would be don't take chances; the lower Severn can be a dangerous place at times, especially when rising. Aside from the fact that white topped waves can appear during storm conditions on its long, exposed straights, the prospect of hitting floating debris or of a submerged tree snagging your anchor rope are situations to be avoided.

River conditions vary, and only by fishing regularly can you build up a full picture. Apart from floods, a rising river is the 'kiss of death' for the zander angler. Equally, prolonged dry spells in winter can provide cold and very clear water, which can be equally frustrating. On some days the pike will switch on and zander are very scarce, and on other days it's the other way around. Bank fishing is a slightly different matter. Assume that the river is within its banks but

coloured and has a powerful flow. A dead loss? Well no, not always, as the zander will tend to move to slack areas, often right at the end of your rod tip on the river shelf. Even then, though, not all areas hold zander; again, river knowledge and swim location remain key. Take care on autumn and winter bank swims as they can be extremely treacherous at times when wet. Only recently I got into a very precarious position when fishing alone, and I only just managed to clamber back up the bank. The swim was fine when I arrived, but the slope became like a ski ramp after only a shower. Some anglers fix a large spike at the top of the bank and attach a climbing rope.

Another factor that can affect the river is an influx of dam water from Lake Vyrnwy and Lynn Clywedog. Cold dam water affecting sport is often quoted as a problem by some anglers, but so many factors come into play on the Severn that I personally don't worry about dam water releases.

Steve Budd with a Severn eleven.

Boat Fishing

The Severn is navigable for around forty-eight miles from Stourport to Gloucester, which encompasses the riverside towns of Worcester, Upton and Tewkesbury, all of which lie in 'zander country'. The towns were once important inland ports for trade, but are now attractive tourist centres.

Putting your boat in the river can be done via a number of slipways but you must have a British Waterways licence, evidence of insurance and pay a launch fee. At present anglers have a good relationship with most other boat users, who take to the river in large numbers in narrow boats, and in pleasure cruisers up to large, ocean-going boats. In addition, River-Boat Shuffles (floating discos) operate above Tewkesbury. During the summer months traffic can be heavy, so you need to know what you are doing. Freight barges are a recent addition to the river; called Perch, Pike and Chub, they transport sand and gravel aggregates between sites just below Upton and down to the M50 bridge.

Parts of the river are routinely dredged to prevent silting up. Grounding your boat should not be an issue, but I did see a cruiser sinking two years ago; the owner decided to pull in to tie up on a bank reinforced with boulders, and was oblivious to the fact that the boulders extended below the waterline. Most fishing boats are shallow draught and this would not be an issue, but take

Ken Lancett with a boat-caught zander of 12lb 10oz.

This fish illustrates the track record of the Severn. It was caught in 1994 and weighed in at an impressive 14lb 2oz.

Steve Budd with his first double of 10lb 4oz.

Steve with a fish of 13lb 2oz.

A lovely zander from the Severn of 13lb 6oz, caught by Ken Lancett.

care to avoid propeller strikes if you have a long-shaft engine and want to pull up onto the marginal shelf.

Potential

As a previous holder of the zander record, the Severn's potential speaks for itself. Many had this venue down as the source of Britain's first twenty-pound zander; this has not happened yet. Indeed, upper double-figure fish are few and far between, and whilst I only hear of a proportion of those caught I would estimate less than a dozen of that size come out each year. Indeed I know many a competent angler who has yet to see a double-figure zander, let alone an upper double.

(Author's note: shortly after this chapter was written, the record was broken and the Severn produced the country's first twenty-pounder at 21lb 6oz. I decided to leave this paragraph in the book rather than re-write, as this shows just how much of a shock the record was, as it was completely out of the blue, and caught by a bream angler on a halibut pellet to boot.)

I firmly believe UK anglers still have a lot to learn and understand about zander, compared to our European friends and US anglers fishing for walleye. As I spend more time in pursuit of zander I find myself torn between a bait or lure approach, which is born from the fact that I have received advice from very good anglers in both camps. Yet when I am specifically targeting the bigger fish I am drawn to lures, which I know will be at odds with Mark Barrett's approach. It would not surprise me in the least to get a call from Dave Pugh to say he had a twenty today…and it's not a pike.

Question and Answer Session on Bait Fishing with Ken Lancet and Steve Budd

Steve Budd is a very experienced Severn zander angler and, in my opinion, Ken Lancet, who has a considerable number of double-figure fish to his name, has the most zander experience on the Severn. I knew before I started to write this section for Mark's book that extracting information from these two would be a tough task, as, like most dedicated specialist anglers, they are loathe to give away free information that they have spent hundreds of hours accumulating by being out there fishing in all the elements. I have set out the result of our chat below, in the form of a question (Q) and answer (A) session.

Q – Given the Severn's known zander potential, and the fact that it previously held the record, why do we not see more zander anglers on the river?

A – Mainly because of the difficulty the water presents to those new to it. Living locally we can pick the better conditions and fish at the right time. Often our better results come from short 2 to 3 hour sessions that are not a feasible option for those travelling any distance. Many newcomers to the river are often only seen for one season before a reality check sets in. Another factor is that the banks are not at all like the Fens, and tend to eliminate the long-stay bivvy angler. Leaving conditions aside, success is really dictated by locating the zander; whilst they may be well spread out when feeding, they are not found on all parts of the river.

In addition, access to much of the river for bank fishing is very limited, resulting in visitors only having Birmingham Angler Associa-

Ken with a 13lb 6oz fish.

A Severn monster of 15lb 2oz.

tion stretches or the free stretch at Uckinghall, for instance.

Q – What amazed me in my first two years purposely fishing for zander was that I often only saw a handful of predator anglers on any one day. Do you see it differently?

A – No, in fact the 2004/05 season saw very few anglers on the river.

Q – Some of my fishing friends feel that floods in recent years have had a knock-on effect with the predators, and we have assumed year classes of silver fish were lost. My own view is that baitfish numbers have reduced for a number of reasons. Do you agree?

A – Actually, no – prey fish appear to be at the usual level along the river, albeit during winter

the 'herring ball' effect is very noticeable. Find the ball and you will find the predators.

Q – Fair enough, but what is true is the change in schoolie numbers. Whereas three to four years ago we could catch numbers of them casting lures, they now appear to have been reduced in number.

A – It's probably a year-class thing and could be noticeably different next year. The river and its fish regularly change in cycles.

Q – I can't avoid the main question – can Ray Armstrong's 18lb 12oz river record be broken, and could the Severn produce Britain's first 20lb zander?

A – Yes to both questions, but it's a while since that fish was caught. The irony is that whilst we

A fat Severn fish of 14lb 10oz.

spend many hours on the river trying to catch the bigger fish, a visitor could get lucky on a one-day visit. Certainly fish over 17lb are very rare, but the potential is always there to catch that exceptional fish. The fish may well be out there already but there are comparatively few anglers actually devoting serious time to their capture.

Q – How would you summarize your fishing methods?

A – We fish from June to March from bank and boat. Legered coarse dead baits tend to be the predominant method on a straight lead rig. We use braid for boat fishing but nylon for the bank, as drop back indicators don't tend to work too well on braid. Line strength is 12 to 15lb nylon and lead sizes from 1½ to 4 oz on occasions.

Q – I note you favour dead baits, which may surprise a few people.

A – Overall that's our preferred choice, and on occasions we have had to dispatch lives to keep catching. Strange but true.

Q – Do you suffer many blanks?

A – It's a fairly rare occurrence, and when it does happen it is usually because the water is warm and clear. From our short session fishing a poor result would be just a couple of fish.

Q – What would you class as your best bait?

A – A toss-up between roach and small skim-mers, live or dead.

Q –What's been your most successful method, and what tackle do you use?

A – The best method is without doubt a simple straight leger rig, no need to over-complicate it. Steve uses Fox 2½lb boat rods for bank and boat fishing together with Shimano 6000 bait-runners. Ken uses 11ft, 2½lb North Western rods, combined with Simano 5000 baitrunners. Line is any good brand in 12lb breaking strain.

Q – What's the largest bait you have had a zander on, and what would be the ideal size?

A – A 14lb 2oz zander that took a 10oz roach live bait whilst pike fishing. Ideal size would be up to 8oz.

Steve holds the zander of many anglers' dreams at 15lb 8oz.

Q – How often do you fish?

A – Steve fishes three to four times a week – Ken more than that!

Q – What's your best ever bag?

A – Two days stand out, the first resulted in three doubles to Ken with the largest weighing 16lb 2oz. On the other day Steve had a brace of 12lb 8oz and 15lb 8oz. Bear in mind, though, that an awful lot of sessions can be undertaken without a double showing up.

Q – Steve, what was your worst moment on the river?

A – I packed up a boat session late one evening and travelled back to base in the dark. Hitting a floating tree at full speed was a wake-up call; the boat rode over the top of the tree but the engine and transom were nearly ripped off in the process. I was very lucky.

Q – I nearly did that myself in daylight with bright sunshine and surface glare. I didn't see the log in the water until the last second. It was very unsettling. I also had a bizarre episode fishing alone a few months ago when a floating bottle 'pinged' along the side of my aluminium boat; it sounded like all the rivets were popping, and until the bottle passed the boat I didn't have a clue what was going on. Any more safety tips, Steve?

A – Fishing after floods requires extreme care. I have fallen in a couple of times, and getting out in winter can be very difficult. It is a very dangerous river in places.

Q – You both know I prefer to lure fish for the zander, but I rarely see either of you using lures; is there a reason for that?

A – We find baits more productive, especially for the above-average fish. That said, Steve had a 10lb 4oz on a large professor spoon.

Q – Contrary to the often-heard phrase 'night time is the right time', I believe you have a dif-

Another Severn monster for Ken of 14lb 15oz – that's honesty!

ferent standpoint when it comes to the Severn.

A – Yes – once the light has completely gone, forget it.

Q – That could be seen as a controversial view to some.

A – So be it. It's based on our countless hours on the river, and that's what we have found.

Q – It's an interesting view and one shared by some other anglers. In discussion with Dave Pugh he suggests that before dark the zander may well lie in their favourite lairs combining depth, structure, flow and light intensity, etc. but as night falls they may well move to other areas on the hunt. There would appear to be no hard and fast rules here.

A – Those views could well be right, and might be worth exploring further. Without doubt location is the key.

Q – Finally, I know both of you moved to Tewkesbury for the fishing. I tried that with my wife, but with no success. Steve you did it recently, how did you manage to convince yours?

A – Well, I travelled from Birmingham regularly for ten years before the move. Finally I swore to her that the move was necessitated by work and a desire for a better quality of life in the country (not fishing).

JC – Yeah right Steve!

Ken Lancet's personal best presently stands at 16lb 3oz, and I suspect that this will increase further in the coming years. Certainly in Steve Budd's case, having moved from Birmingham to Tewkesbury, the brace of 15lb+ zander in his first year has justified the dedication he has shown.

5 STILLWATER ZANDER

These days, most zander anglers equate zander with rivers or the Fen drains. However, the history of British zander has seen a few stillwater stockings, long before the ninety-seven zander that were the basis of the zander population as we know it these days. However, most of these were isolated, or never really established themselves, but since then many still waters have received zander that have gone on to produce a thriving, sustained zander population. Woburn Abbey, for instance, received zander as far back as the nineteenth century. These fish survived and bred, and established a population within the water that survives to the present day.

Elsewhere, most still waters that have established zander populations have done so through legal stocking of zander, through natural introduction because of flooding, or through illegal

A view of Roswell Pits.

introductions. Throughout the Great Ouse valley there are a number of lakes and gravel pits that have populations of zander. These were gained either through having a direct link to the river, as in the case of Roswell Pits and Wyboston Lakes, or through the effects of flooding. Pits that fall into this latter category include the St Ives Lagoon, Drayton Fen and Swavesey Lake.

Unquestionably, these fish have done very well in a stillwater environment. Roswell Pits, for instance, has a large head of zander, and they are of a good average size. It has also held the record for zander for quite some time, only losing its crown to the River Severn. However, Roswell has had a population for a considerable time as it is situated not too far upstream of Denver sluice where the zander were introduced. Therefore the population has had time to settle, helped in part by the fact that Roswell has very shallow, coloured water, with large numbers of rudd, bleak, roach, etc. that the zander can prey upon. Roswell also has a large population of bream, a species that seems to

attract zander like a magnet. Due to all of these factors its quite possible to draw conclusions as to the impact of zander colonization upon a still water.

As was seen in the rivers and drains, the initial impact of zander upon the prey fish was to reduce numbers, though never as drastically as was claimed by some. However, the populations soon recovered and the zander found their niche within the predator biomass. In reality, as far as Roswell was concerned, this was by displacing the resident pike to some extent. Up to then the pike had been the apex predator, and with the water still recovering from perch disease, as many were in the 1960s and 1970s, there was little in the way of competition for the new arrivals. Nowadays Roswell still holds good populations of smaller prey species, as well as good numbers of pike, perch and zander.

Other pits in the Ouse valley have not seen the boom in zander numbers that Roswell did, because the environment wasn't as suitable as

Ollie Newman with a Roswell zander caught trolling.

that at Roswell. Most of the gravel pits in the Ouse valley are very rich in weed growth, and the water quality is excellent, as can be seen from the specimen fish of other species that these lakes produce. The water is also gin clear, and this doesn't really suit the zander's preference for coloured water and low light levels. Another reason why the zander population has not really taken off is the impact upon the prey fish of the cormorant explosion. The pits of the Ouse valley offered the cormorants ideal hunting opportunities, and because they have safe sanctuary at Hitchingbrooke Country Park the decimation of the roach and rudd in the lakes around the area has been almost total. This has meant that the only fish left in numbers in the lakes are those that were too big for the cormorants to prey upon, and therefore also too big for the zander. Despite this, the pits have produced some very big zander. St Ives has produced zander well into double figures, whilst the pits at Drayton have also produced some double-figure zander.

Further up the river system, around the St Neots area, Wyboston Lakes have been known for their quality zander for some time. These lakes are like Roswell in that they are joined to the main river, but unlike Roswell they offer the zander very different conditions from the local river. The lakes at Wyboston are relatively deep, up to 12ft, and are usually well-tinged with colour. However, the nearby river is quite shallow and very clear, more suitable to barbel and chub than zander. I have fished the river in this area for many years for perch, mainly using live bait, and have yet to catch one from the river. Friends of mine have fished it for even longer and have caught very few fish, though one of their guests did once take a 12lb 8oz fish from the river fairly close to the pits' entrance.

Moving away from the Fens there are many other still waters that contain zander. Among the more famous of these are Old Bury Hill Lakes at Dorking in Surrey, Frisby Pits in Leicestershire, Stanborough Lakes in Hertfordshire and Tyram Hall in Doncaster. In all of these lakes, except Old Bury Hill, the zander have suffered from persecution from the controlling clubs, and still

Mark Smith with a double-figure zander from the smallest of Roswell Pits.

do, though that situation has changed recently at Frisby. Realistically, as has been seen time and time again, this persecution does little to reduce the numbers of zander in a water; in fact it could easily be argued that the attempts at eradicating the species have in fact just exacerbated the problem, as the bigger fish will be in part self-predating, and if left they will help to keep the number of zander in check. Certainly when the cull was implemented on the Fen rivers in the 1980s, the end result was an explosion of smaller zander. I can well remember catching upwards of fifteen zander in a day, yet my personal best at that time only weighed a little over 3lb.

The one lake where zander have been viewed as a positive asset is at Old Bury Hill. Here zander

A view over Swavesey Lake, which has in common with many of the Ouse valley pits a low head of big zander.

are treated with the utmost respect, to the extent that courses are instigated in how to both catch, and handle the zander, all under the guidance of their resident predator expert Eric Bailey. This has resulted in some great zander fishing being available to anglers in the south of the country for whom the trip up to the Fens may just be too far. Old Bury Hill has produced some very big zander, to a venue best of 16lb 2oz, but is perhaps better known as a water that produces numbers of fish to around the 14lb mark. It does, though, offer the zander angler the chance to fish afloat from one of the estate's many punts. This offers the zander angler a chance to fish some different methods more effectively, such as drifter-float fishing, or vertical jigging.

The last of the famous zander still waters are Coombe Abbey Lakes in Coventry and Ferry Meadows in Peterborough.

Coombe has a massive reputation amongst zander anglers as it has produced some amazing zander over the years. The current best for Coombe stands at 19lb and was caught by local legend Bob Moreton. This fish really shook the record books and has been backed up by some other fish in the 17lb range. A lot of the fishing at Coombe has historically been done at very long range, often by the use of remote-controlled boats. I have to say that this certainly wouldn't be a method of fishing that I would enjoy, as the use of boats has always been a topic with which I am not particularly enamoured. However, personal issues aside, fishing at this type of range will require extra thought from the angler. The use of braid as a mainline is an absolute must (one of the very few situations in zandering where I would recommend its use). Also, heavier indicators will be needed to register drop-back-type bites at the sort of ranges that can be fished by boat. However, boats do offer the chance to present live bait undamaged at range, so they do have their uses.

Ferry meadows are another type of water where extreme range fishing, again by boats, has been used to great effect. Ferry meadows have never really had the reputation for outsized zander, but they certainly produce a good number of double-figure fish every year. They probably suffer in the ultimate size stakes, simply because their coloured water offers the zander such favourable feeding that the zander population is numerous.

Stillwater zander are still something of a novelty in the UK, though that situation will almost certainly change over the course of time. In common with a lot of records, I fully expect that in the not too distant future the biggest zander will be found in the rich gravel pits of the south and east. All these waters will provide the zander angler with interesting diversions, and ultimately with a new and exciting challenge.

The author with a brace of stillwater zander.

6 LOCATING YOUR PREY: THE COMFORT ZONE

You may think this a strange phrase in a fishing book; however, in this chapter I will explain why being in the comfort zone will only help you to catch more zander from the Fens in daylight.

So what do I mean by the comfort zone? Put simply, it's finding those areas that zander frequent, primarily in the daytime, and primarily when they are not actively hunting for prey. But going into the comfort zone is more than just that. Location is of course always number one in any angling situation, as you cannot catch what is not there, but can you get what is there to accept bait? After all, when you are fishing for zander that are not hunting, you are in theory trying to catch fish that have either been feeding already, in the hours of darkness, or have eaten days before and are digesting a meal. Logic tells you that these fish will be harder to catch. However, with a bit of thought it's very easy to use the fish's own feeding instincts against it.

Factors to look out for are:

- cover from predators and flow;
- light values;
- proximity to food;
- security.

Flow and light levels will play a huge part in a zander's hunting activities.

We are looking for areas where a pack of, or a single, zander can lay up for the times when they are at a distinct disadvantage in hunting. To put that another way, the zander, as we know, is adapted to feed at night or in times of low light levels. Therefore at those times the predator has a distinct advantage over its prey and hunting is likely to provide better returns against energy spent than in times of gin-clear water and strong sunlight, when the prey are able to see the predator too easily.

Understanding this basic principle is fundamental to determining your own water's 'comfort zones'. Other factors that will vary from water to water also need to be considered. Flow rates, whether by nature or artificial pumping, will play a large part, so too will water clarity and time of year, depth of water, overhead cover and venue topography and temperature. Less important in my opinion is availability of prey fish, at least in the immediate vicinity. Obviously the zander will not be miles away from their prey; however, neither are they likely to be right in the middle of them as of course this would move the prey.

Comfort zones can also be very small, defined areas, yet can hold large numbers of fish of all sizes and, once identified, can prove to be very consistent spots, although very different from a pike hotspot as its not an area that a zander goes to to feed, rather to lay up for the day.

So taking into account all those factors we need to find such areas, and in turn to catch the zander present. I will start with a little story that appeared in a recent Zander Angling Club magazine, the *Snapper*. One of the members is a keen diver and regularly dives a lake that holds just one zander. On daytime dives the zander was always found in the same area, above or around a sunken car. The zander was very docile and would stand a fair degree of interaction with the divers. Whenever they dived in the day, there would be the zander round his own little vehicle. However, the picture changed on a night dive. On such occasions the zander could be found swimming around anywhere but where the car was. To me this is the best possible example I could provide of a comfort zone. The zander almost certainly chose the car as

it offered a degree of sanctuary from predators; if it needed to the zander could swim inside for top cover, and the car was in a deep part of the lake, so light intensity would have been toward the lowest in that water.

The idea that the light was at its lowest *respective to that water* is a very important factor to consider, and is fundamental to understanding the theory. After all, not every water is coloured, and in fact for longer and longer periods of the year these days water clarity in the Fens can be very good. In times such as these the zander will choose different areas in which to lie up. Areas that come into their own in situations like this are those with top cover. That can take the form of natural cover, such as lilies, undercuts and overhanging trees, or man-made cover, such as bridges. In the summer and in clear water conditions it is areas such as these that I will look at first. I have seen more than a few zander taken from around lily beds in particular in the summer. In fact my friend Ollie's best-ever zander of 10lb 12oz was taken from underneath lilies when the temperature was well into the eighties. In warmer water zander will be quite prepared to come into very shallow water, such as where lilies grow, to find such spots.

On another water that I fished regularly I identified two specific comfort zones. This water is predominantly very shallow, with depths of 4 to 5ft being the norm, and is always slightly coloured. Lily beds are common but only one such bed had a comfort zone. The reason for this was that in this particular bed there was an undercut bank, which dropped a further foot in depth. Further along from this spot was another zone, this one very different. Again it was not very far from the bank but was in an area that was difficult to access from the bank. However, it could easily be reached from a boat. Here the zone consisted of average depth water, but it had two fallen trees in the swim, though there was little left of either. This small area always held zander and was often used as a day-saver swim. The presence of the snags on an otherwise barren stretch gave the zander an area where they could hold up comfortably for the day.

Ollie Newman with the 10lb 12oz zander taken in 80 degree heat.

As the season wears on different factors will determine a comfort zone.

The third zone on that water was far subtler and was only identified by use of an echo sounder (or plumbing equipment). It was a gentle depth variation, dropping off quite sharply from 4ft to 6ft, so it represented some of the deepest water on the venue. Trolling baits over this spot was almost always guaranteed to produce takes, and in common with such zones the sport was usually hectic. Four to eight fish could be taken from any of the zones mentioned, my best result coming from the tree zone where I took fish over 6lb to a best of 10lb 12oz in an hour. Catches like that may be special, but they are by no means uncommon. Just bear in mind what constitutes a comfort zone. On the last water mentioned, flow was not a consideration, but on some waters it is probably the major consideration, particularly as the year wears on.

Even with flow, though, we need to bear in mind the key phrase *respective to the water*, as flow rates and refuges will differ from water to water. Two examples of extreme differences in waters are the Old West and the Great Ouse, though in effect they are actually one and the same. Now the Old West is shallow (5ft on average), whereas the Great Ouse is around twelve feet, down to twenty feet or more along parts of its ten-mile bank. Both waters are dotted with marinas, some good for fishing, some not so good. They both also flow well in the winter in times of flood, the Ouse more so than the Old West. The Ouse also has many areas of slack water, and long, sweeping bends that offer steadier water.

The Old West has little in the way of refuge from abnormal flow, and as such the comfort zones are far easier to identify, as they are so few and far between. The Ouse has far more and therefore they take more tracking down, but of

Marinas are a definite hotspot or comfort zone in the winter or during heavy floods.

A marina-caught nine pounder taken by the author on a very small bait.

course they are there. We need to look for any variation in flow, preferably slacker water, creases in the flow and of course the completely slack water in off-cuts or marinas.

One important thing to consider with slack water is the relationship of the water's average depth to that of the slack water. If the water is dramatically shallower than the main channel, then in my experience they will not be zander-friendly. This applies a lot on the Ouse where the marinas can be just a few feet deep, whereas the river is 12ft+. The shallow water will at times be considerably affected by temperature rise and drop, so much so that zander tend to give these areas a miss. However, on the Old West, there are areas of slack water that are shallower than the main river yet these hold zander because the difference is much less pronounced, only being a

foot or so shallower. In addition there is far less choice for the fish on the river, which is always an important factor to consider. On other waters there may not even be the choice of features like a marina.

Many Fen drains are by reputation completely straight, featureless waterways. Never has such a myth had such an airing. There are always features that will be some form of refuge, the commonest being change of depth (drop offs) and bends. Some supposedly dead straight drains will have quite dramatic bends; they just need to be found. When they are, these are very hot areas. There's little in the way of choice and, needs must, zander will take up residence. Sudden changes in depth are other good floodwater/ river zones. Despite the fact that we have on the whole talked about zander getting out of the

Using tiny baits can be the key to consistent catching in the daytime.

flow, they actually are quite able to deal with very strong flow, as has been seen by the success of the species in the Severn and Avon in the Midlands. However, to fight flow all day long will use a huge amount of energy and to refuel the zander will need to eat more, so it does make them easier to catch.

So far I have covered factors that combine to create a comfort zone, but how do I go about catching these fish? After all they are, in effect, not feeding but resting up for the night ahead. In this instance I use the 'After Eights syndrome' to catch them. What do I mean by this? Well, picture the scene, you have just finished the usual Christmas lunch, have feasted on turkey and Christmas pudding, and couldn't eat another thing – that is until the After Eight mints come out and suddenly you find you can just manage something more. I use the same principle to catch zander. This means using far smaller baits than I would normally use, 2oz being an absolute maximum. The zander sees the food and, although not actively hunting, it cannot resist this easy snack to keep its energy levels up. Now this may be wishful thinking, but I can only say that it works for me, my friends and clients, and has done for many years. Method is immaterial, though a simple free-roving bait can be deadly in this situation, proving that extra bit of freedom is an irresistible draw to a dormant predator.

7 ZANDER AND BREAM

Ask any long-term zander angler where would be the first place that they would look for a really big zander, and I bet that 90 per cent of them would answer 'Around the bream shoals.' Why zander should follow bream shoals has always been a source of conjecture. Although we may never know the reason, it doesn't stop anglers from having a theory about it, and I am no different to the rest.

That zander go with bream shoals is taken as lore these days, and quite rightly so in my opinion. I have taken enough good zander catches, both big individual captures and strings of fish, to know that bream are a good indicator of zander being present. In fact some friends and myself took the biggest run of doubles that we have taken from any one area, from an area where I had located the bream on Ten Mile Bank. In the

A scenic shot of a known Ouse bream area.

A 10lb 10oz zander for Paul Barrett, from the week where we found the bream and really cashed in.

Glenn Gillett got in on the act too with a 12lb 12oz fish.

space of a week zander of 14lb 2oz, 12lb 12oz, 11lb 7oz, 10lb 10oz and 10lb, plus four 9lb fish and numerous lesser fish, were taken from a stretch of bank no more than 80yd long. The only reason that the sport ended was that at the end of the week the rains came and this moved the bream, taking the zander off with them.

So the correlation between bream shoals and zander is undisputed, but what are the possible reasons for this unlikely pairing?

I have heard a few different theories, but my own is as follows. I believe that the zander follow the bream because feeding bream cause an awful lot of disturbance to the strata of the bottom, usually resulting in a clouding up of the water. Now I don't particularly think that the coloured water in itself is the reason, even though, with its superior eyesight, the zander would be at an advantage to hunt members of the shoal. If this was the case the zander may come unstuck, in that the shoals that zander tend to hunt around are quite big bream, in the 2lb and upward class. To eat a 2lb bream whole would take some zander. Rather, I think that as the bream go on the feed, the disturbed bottom releases fine particles of food upwards, over the shoal members, food that the smaller fish, such as roach, skimmers, etc. are quick to cash in on. Anybody who has watched fish in a frenzy of feeding will be well aware that their natural caution is abandoned and feeding becomes the all-important function. Coupled with coloured water around the bream, this provides the zander with an opportunity to slip in under cover and launch attacks on the unsuspecting prey fish – all of which makes a zander's ideal hunting situation.

I have also heard the theory that the zander team up and attack a member of the shoal, all taking chunks out of the unfortunate victim until it is incapacitated, whereupon the zander devour it en masse. Personally I hold no truck with this idea, for several reasons. First, there is no evidence of zander hunting in an organized manner. Sure, they do hunt in packs, but there is more evidence that the feeding is a free-for-all. Certainly on the very rare occasions that I have witnessed zander hunting there is more evidence of frenzy,

with zander coming out of the water in their eagerness to get at food in shallow water. Second, I do not believe that the zander is capable of feeding in that manner. They are equipped to hunt in a manner whereby they first disable their prey and then swallow it hole. I don't believe that a zander is physically capable of tearing chunks out of a fish. It is true that zander have very powerful jaws, but they do not have the serrated teeth necessary to slash and tear food. Their teeth are designed to puncture and wound their prey sufficiently for them to line them up for swallowing whole.

I know that there are stories of anglers seeing zander with bream and other large prey cornered and looking for the world like they are waiting to pounce, but my interpretation of this behaviour is similar to that of a cat and a mouse. The prey fish fascinates the zander and their hunting instinct has been turned on; however, this action is more that of curiosity than a definite attempt at feeding. For those who doubt this, just look at the way a fish's natural curiosity is used to precipitate its downfall, particularly in the carp and lure fishing worlds. After all, carp anglers catch fish on bits of plastic and rubber that bear no resemblance to anything they are likely to encounter naturally. Of course, as fish have no hands they only have their mouths to test if something is edible or not. I believe that this behaviour is purely curiosity.

Another point worth considering in relation to zander following bream shoals, which is often overlooked, is that the main thing that both species have in common is a nocturnal feeding habit. Most fish are active at night; however, bream, and in particular the bigger specimens, are very much nocturnal feeders to the extent that, unlike most other fish, the bulk of their feeding takes place in darkness. Looking at all the facets of bream – feeding at night, colouring the water when they feed and disturbing food for other fish, is it really surprising that zander follow the shoals?

Of course, knowing that zander follow bream is one thing, using that information to catch them is something else. I don't know of too many zander anglers who are also keen bream anglers, so outside help is going to be needed, along with the tell-tale visual signs.

Some stretches of rivers and drains are well-known bream hotspots. I can think of areas of the Ouse and the Cut Off Channel in particular that have been known as good bream pegs for many years. Of course, the bream are not always in evidence; maybe, like zander, they use these areas for their resting point during the day. Whatever the reason, the bream are undoubtedly known to feed in these areas and you can count on there being zander somewhere close by.

Another good way to locate the bream is to study the local match results. Usually these will give exact peg numbers as well as venues, and can be an invaluable aid. The only drawback is that in these days of heavily stocked commercial fisheries, fewer match anglers are fishing the rivers. Even in the area where I live the matches on rivers become fewer year-on-year, a bit ironic really as I have not seen prey fish populations at this level in all of the drains and rivers for a good few years.

Of course bream can also be tracked down by visual means. In very clear water the discolouration of the water makes it possible to see where they are feeding. However, on most of the drains and rivers I fish, this is not possible as boat traffic

The second of Paul Barrett's brace at 11lb 7oz.

I managed this one of 9lb 10oz, but better was to come...

keeps the water coloured all year round. Bream will show themselves regularly by 'porpoising' on the top of the water as they roll. The only drawback to this is that bream that are showing in this way are invariably travelling from feeding area to area, and not actually in the process of feeding. I know a few anglers that have caught numbers of zander by leapfrogging along with the bream as they move, but in my experience this is rather more a chance thing. What I mean is that it's difficult to predict where a bream shoal is going to start travelling. It is usually more of a serendipitous affair, in that the angler either spots them on arriving at the venue, or that the bream arrive when the angler is already set up. Of course this should always be taken advantage of, if at all possible, though it may be difficult to leapfrog all the assorted paraphernalia involved in night fishing.

Of course, once you really get to know a water, you may be able to predict where the bream will show, though I wish you luck in doing so, as they do tend to change on a regular basis.

One of the tactics that I use to locate bream is to drive the drains finding out what the pleasure anglers have caught. I used this tactic to track down the spot mentioned earlier on Ten Mile Bank on the Ouse. The day in question was a Sunday in November and, as it was still mild, the match/pleasure anglers were still very much in evidence, though despite driving many miles from Ely to Ten Mile Bank none had caught very much, and no one had caught bream. Finally I stumbled upon a man fishing with his young son, who had caught several decent sized bream and was just packing up. Whilst I stood talking to him I worked out where he had been casting his

The pick of the bunch at 14lb 2oz.

Bream, I love them!

feeder (usually on the Ouse most feeder anglers fish about a third of the way across the river), so the positioning for one of the rods was sorted straight away. After the man and his son had left I moved into his swim and during the course of the night I landed several zander up to a personal best weight of 14lb 2oz.

One final thing worth mentioning with respect to the link between bream and zander is the fact that the zander that are around the shoals tend to be bigger than on average, and are usually 8lb or more. I believe this behaviour is a learned trait rather than a natural reaction. The zander come across feeding bream during their life and some learn to follow the shoals to get some easy pickings, whilst others do not seem to pick up on this opportunity. The fish that do follow bream grow large, while the other fish have to work that bit harder to find food and don't grow so quickly or as big, ultimately, as the shoal followers.

Before you dismiss this theory, remember that of the waters in the Fens with the track record for producing large zander (I am thinking here of places such as the Middle Level, Great Ouse, Old Bedford/Delph, Relief Channel and Roswell Pits), all of them bar the Ouse and Old Bedford/Delph have produced record zander in the past, and all of them have or have had large stocks of bream. If you compare that with other Fen rivers where the Bream are either in small numbers or pretty much non-existent, such as the Lark, Little Ouse, Forty Foot and Old West, the top weight for zander is much lower. Further evidence, if it is needed, can be provided by looking at Roswell Pits. The pits used to have the reputation of being a superb bream fishery, and I can remember watching huge shoals of bream rolling there when I used to fish the pits a lot. Of course during that time Roswell produced Bob Meadows' record zander of 18lb 8oz. In recent years the bream fishing at Roswell has gone into decline and there hasn't been, to my knowledge, a zander over 15lb out of there for several years. Coincidence? I will leave it up to the reader to decide, but in the mean time I am off to find myself a shoal of bream.

8 LANDING, HANDLING AND PHOTOGRAPHY

It is fair to say that within zander angling there is probably a higher percentage of missed runs or takes than with the other predatory species. There are also probably just as many theories and conjecture as to why this should be so and what can be done to improve hook up rates. I have my own thoughts about this, born of many years of agonizing over the problem.

The most likely cause of dropped or missed runs – schoolie zander.

Taking the Bait

Let's start with the issue of zander being finicky with baits. It is an established part of zander angling that you will suffer from a higher percentage of dropped or missed runs than with pike, but this is where the inexperienced zander angler starts to think that their presentation is at fault and that they need to use smaller hooks as the zander are feeling the hooks. I don't think this is the case. In my opinion, backed up by years of zander fishing, it is more down to the zander's different hunting technique to pike, and to the way in which a zander will swallow a bait. Most people's predator angling experience in the UK is with pike, so the way that they react and their continual point of reference for predator fishing is pike. They may therefore approach zander expecting to find they feed the same way as pike. Zander are similar, but very different, which may sound contrary but is well worth remembering.

Whereas a pike will take bait across the flanks before turning and swallowing, a zander cannot feed in that way. For a start a zander's front canine teeth are designed to stab and inflict enough injury to a prey fish to disable it so the zander can line up and swallow it. In the act of the stab that the zander performs to disable its prey its front bottom canine teeth locate into sockets intermeshed with the front top canine teeth – effectively they interlock. This means that the zander cannot swallow bait whilst those front teeth are embedded in the prey. To swallow it has to release the prey fish first, and at this juncture things differ again from pike. Pike always swallow bait head first; zander will swallow bait in either direction, head or tail first. Of course, that is providing they get hold of the bait a second time. I have caught so many prey species with zander marks in them to realize that they are far from a super-efficient predator.

The zander's feeding technique affects the angler in a couple of ways. Of course there is the fact that at some stage in the take, particularly with live baits, the zander is going to let go. Now with a poorly timed strike, bang out of the zander's mouth goes the bait and hooks. Furthermore, on that initial strike and stab it is quite conceivable that the hooks are nowhere near the mouth, as the zander will be hitting just about anywhere to disable the prey, though I would say that the rear of the fish is the favoured area. With a pike we know that the initial pick-up point is going to be along the flank, so hooks can be positioned accordingly. The same situation just isn't possible with a zander, so we have to accept that at times hook positioning will work against us, and making those hooks smaller won't make any difference, nor will it make a zander swallow a bait at a point where it is physically incapable of doing so.

I ought to clarify that I am talking about the use of live bait rather than dead. I think that zander on the whole give stronger runs on dead bait than on live, simply because there is no need for the initial stab. Having said that, you still have the over-ambitious schoolies to deal with, so dead baits are far from foolproof. In fact, due to their inertness, dead baits are far less size-discriminating than live. I have had average zander on some very big dead baits. One that comes to mind in particular was a seven-pounder from the Relief Channel, which picked up a 10oz dead roach; in a live bait I wouldn't expect a fish of that size to take the bait, another reason why I prefer lives over deads.

There is also a preconception that scaling down tackle and bait size will help to hook up more runs. There is an element of truth here, in that smaller baits will make hooking runs easier

This head-on shot of a 9lb Ouse zander clearly shows the very small mouth of a zander in comparison to its body, and of course in comparison to a pike, making hitting runs sometimes an issue.

because they provide a bait that the schoolies can easily take, but therein lies the play-off. Do you want to have a chance of everything that comes along, from 1lb to 15lb, or do you want to catch those fish of 5lb and above? Personally I no longer want to catch tiny schoolies, and I really don't see why anyone particularly would. Zander, after all, are not the strongest fighters most of the time, so what is the point in hauling in a 2lb zander on the right equipment, or more pertinently what is the point in endangering the bigger zander, and indeed pike, by trying to make small zander fight harder?

Unhooking and Returning

Once you have got your zander on the bank you are then going to have to deal with the whole unhooking and returning/retention process.

Zander are quite notorious for being far from hardy when caught, and I have personally found this to be the case, particularly in the warmer weather. The lower the rate of dissolved oxygen in the water, the more likely that the zander will have problems on return. In this situation it is imperative that the angler should take as little time as possible in both the playing of the zander, unhooking it and photographing it. In warmer weather I will unhook zander under 10lb in the net, keep it in the water and release it straight away, wherever possible. Even if the fish is required for a photograph, I give it plenty of time to recover first in the net, before being taken from the water.

In the colder weather the dissolved oxygen rate in the water is much higher and usually there are less problems with zander either swallowing baits on the spot, or struggling upon return. However, this is no excuse for poor or sloppy fish handling – it is incumbent upon us all to look after the fish that we catch.

Unhooking zander can be a problem for the uninitiated, particularly for those that are more used to unhooking pike. For starters, there is far less room to work in with a zander than a pike, as they have far smaller mouths. On the plus side, though, there are far fewer teeth to avoid! Zander also have a habit upon capture of puffing out their gills in much the same way that perch do, and clamping their jaws shut. Because zander are designed to stab and disable prey, their jaws are extremely powerful and can be difficult to open when they have done this. To get around this the easiest way to open the jaws is as follows:

Holding a zander the correct way to aid recovery.

1. Take hold of the zander through the gill cover, in the same way you would for pike.
2. Gently insert your forceps into the zander's mouth, taking care not to damage its teeth.
3. Open the forceps up and gently ease back on the jaw at the same time, and the zander's mouth will open up.
4. Removing the hooks is then just the same as with a pike; you can go in either through the mouth or the gills to get to the hooks.

Once the zander is unhooked it can then either be returned or photographed as is required. If photos are being taken and the weather is warm, resting the fish for a while in a net is very worthwhile.

Photographing Zander

Certain issues arise when photographing zander that are not so significant with other species. When the photos are being taken make sure that the fish is held as low as possible, preferably over an unhooking mat, or over thick grass at least. Being a very pale coloured fish the zander can

James Carter about to remove the hooks from a small zander.

This photo shows the bleaching effect that can occur with some cameras when the definition is lost on the flanks of the fish. When the fish in the picture is your first over 12lb it's doubly annoying.

reflect a flash very easily at night. This causes a flaring effect, which will mean that your photo will lack definition. The best way to avoid this is to either move a bit further back from the subject and use the zoom on the camera for framing, or to not take the photo from directly in front of the fish, but more from an angle.

Because the zander's eyes have a light-reflecting surface it is also very important to ensure that your camera has a red eye reduction facility on it, and that you use it. Whilst it is possible with modern digital software packages to rectify this after the event, to my mind the results are never quite the same.

Choice of camera will be very much a personal thing, according to one's preferences and budget. Personally I use two different cameras for my fishing photos. I use a Canon Powershot G5 camera most of the time for my fishing photographs. At the time of writing these have been

out of production for a year or so, but can be bought for a reasonable price on online auction sites or through the forums of angling sites. Buy the biggest lens size that you can afford (if it's a compact), and ensure the camera has a decent self-take facility and ideally a screen that flips out from the camera body and rotates. And of course reliability is a key factor. In my experience Canon cameras have all of the above. I use an EOS 500 camera for the rare occasion that I use slide or print film and, as mentioned, the G series for digital photographs. The G series cameras are particularly good for anglers as they have both a flip-round screen and an infra red remote control that allows you to take the pictures from in front of the camera. This aside, they also produce stunning results in all modes of operation, from landscape to macro.

When composing a shot it's very easy to make a simple mistake that will ruin the photo. In the

The problem of reflection from a zander's eye can be clearly seen in this photo of an Old West ten-pounder.

photo right you will see a good example of this, where an otherwise great shot has been spoiled by the fact that a pole appears to be growing from the angler's head! It is especially difficult to take well-composed photographs at night, when the background will be less obvious. The best type of background to use is some kind of vegetation. This allows the internal metering system on the camera to set on something that is reasonably constant. Vegetation will also be slightly darker and make the fish stand out, which will also allow the colours to be more vivid. Avoid, wherever you can, taking photos with the sky as a background (particularly relevant if you take photographs at the top of river or drain flood banks), or even the water. Whilst the water can be compensated for by using the flash, the sky is not so easy and will result in the subject being very dark. Of course, the further advantage of taking your photograph against the vegetation is that no one else will be able to tell where you caught your fish from.

If I am fishing alone I will set up the tripod beforehand and get everything ready to take a photo (bar the camera). It's then simply a case of attaching the camera and using the remote to frame up the picture, and away you go. In company photography should be even easier, but it's time well spent to first show the other person how to use the

Incorrect framing is displayed perfectly in this picture, with a pole seeming to grow from Ollie Newman's head.

The number plate on the car in the background completely ruined this photo of my 14lb 2oz Ouse zander.

The bank stick method, used to retain exhausted zander for long periods.

camera. On my G series the type of photo (landscape, portrait, macro, aperture priority, etc.), is decided by a twist dial on the top of the camera. It has been known for my friends in the past to inadvertently knock this switch round if they have been particularly ham-fisted. This can lead to photographs being ruined if you do not check them quickly before slipping the fish back, or making sure that they check the dials first.

Retaining zander is something of a controversial subject amongst zander anglers. Some will never retain a zander, whilst others have no qualms about doing so. Personally, I fall between the two camps, in that in no circumstances will I retain zander in the warmer months, but in a Queenford tube, landing net or pike tube, I will retain fish for a short period in the winter. My favoured method is to use the landing net. I use a very big round net that is produced by Wychwood for pike fishing. I favour the round nets for two reasons. First, if there is weed or lilies in the near margin, a triangular net can be difficult to push through, as the draw cord will get caught up. Second, a round net allows a fish that is retained within it to move around far more freely. With zander this is a major issue as the pectoral and pelvic fins are where the fish gets its balance. If these fins are impeded in any way the zander will roll over onto its back, which can lead to its death. Even triangular nets can impede these fins, and carp sacks should never be used, for the same reason.

Once you have finished with the fish it should be returned as soon as possible from whence it came. Even at this stage the angler can encounter problems if care is not taken. Zander are notorious for rolling over onto their back when returned if they have not sufficiently regained their strength. To that end it is important to grip the tail of the fish firmly until it breaks free strongly. Usually this can be seen, as the zander will wave its balancing fins until it shoots forward and away. Unfortunately there will be the odd fish that will seemingly not regain its strength and will need a great deal of nursing on the angler's part to enable it to swim off. On occasion this will be far longer than the angler can devote to it. The trick devised by zander anglers to circumnavigate this problem is to prop the zander up in the margins via three bank sticks. Two of these are placed alongside the zander's flanks just behind the pelvic fins, the third one going in front of the fish. Exhausted fish can often lie in this position for many hours, only to power off when fully recovered.

Obviously the main focus of any zander angler is to put fish on the bank. But making sure that the quarry that we pursue goes back into the water healthy and strong, to provide another angler with the same pleasure that it has given us, is something that should be at the forefront of all our thinking.

9 LURE FISHING

Dave Pugh

I was delighted that Dave Pugh agreed to contribute this chapter, as no one spends more time with lures than Dave. Fishing the Severn and Avon, he has built up a detailed knowledge of the riverbed, flows and features and it is no surprise to me that he has two upper double-figure zander to 16lb+ to his name on lures. I suspect there is a bigger one out there with Dave's name on it – time will tell.

Introduction

I caught my first zander in March 1993 on the Warwickshire Avon near Wick. At 6lb 3oz it was a welcome catch. It took a spinnerbait. Over the next few years I caught a few more on various lures, including a 9lb 5oz fish from the Severn near Tewkesbury. They were still very much bonus catches and I only found one place where I could catch them with any regularity, and not many at that. Then in 2001 I made contact through my website with Michel Huigevoort, from Waalwijk in southern Holland. I went to visit Michel and learned that zander were routinely caught there with jigs and trolled crankbaits. It took me a while to get my tackle sorted out properly before I started to make regular catches myself on the Avon and Severn. In general zander are easy to catch with lures and in some respects are a more reliable target than pike, and although there are still some questions I haven't resolved I am always very confident that when I go zander fishing I'm going to catch some.

I have virtually no experience of bait fishing

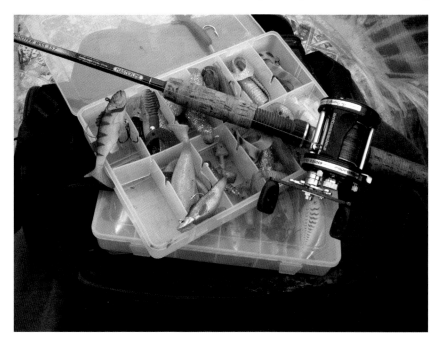

A selection of zander lures ready for keeping mobile.

for zander, but obviously I read about it and I talk to anglers out on the river who use bait, and there are some important differences between the lure angling and bait angling approach that I will highlight in this chapter.

There is no doubt that, for lure fishing, having a boat makes a huge difference to your results. For zander fishing with lures on big rivers it is pretty much essential. There are some swims that I can fish successfully from the bank but the vast majority of my fish come from the boat. It's mainly down to lure control. You can be very precise from the boat – and precise lure control really does matter – but when you are stuck on the bank the shape of the riverbed, snags and the current make it a difficult prospect. You will never match boat-fishing results from the bank, even in the same swims.

Location

Now to those swims. Here the first difference between lure and bait fishing is already apparent; I am expecting to cover a lot of swims in a session, taking fish from many of them. But there will very rarely be more than two or three fish in each spot. I'll cover the spot then move on. This may be purely a daytime phenomenon, but the key to location is speed of flow and depth combined with light penetration. For a zander to be comfortable it needs to find the right combination of light and flow. The perfect swim is on a bend, where there is a gradient of both flow and depth increasing towards the outside of the bend. Somewhere on this feature there will be spots where a few zander will be comfortable, and with experience I've noted some very tight spots

Dave Pugh with an average lure-caught zander.

in these areas that seem to hold a fish as often as not, but in general you have to cover the whole swim thoroughly.

Other factors can be very important; the shade from a bridge will hold fish even if the flow is not apparently sufficient, but the best feature, nearly guaranteeing the presence of zander, is a bridge with pilings in the water. These are rare on the Severn because engineers have generally preferred to span the river in one arch rather than trust the pilings to the Severn floods. The way the current is deflected by a piling makes for a current speed gradient again, and somewhere there will be a spot that the zander like. Even slightly varying flows move these spots and the light penetration also has its effect so you have to search thoroughly to find them sometimes.

Choice of Techniques

There are two choices of technique – either trolling crankbaits, or vertical jigging. If trolling is permitted then it is a fast track to locating swims. Just a few trips will soon build up a list of areas where zander have shown. They will almost invariably be hard-bottomed areas, and quite often when trolling with the crankbait bumping the riverbed the sudden change to a harder bottom – signalled by the rod tip jarring more fiercely as the lure's lip bumps over stones or hard clay – is accompanied almost immediately by a take; mark these spots where the riverbed changes, the zander love them.

I'll discuss precise choice of crankbait later. Most people see trolling as a lazy method. I can only imagine that they either have not tried it, or have tried it and done it badly. The most difficult part of trolling crankbaits is getting the speed right. In general I go fast, much faster than anyone else I've seen trolling. The rod should be bent well around and you will be concentrating very hard on trying to watch the sonar and where you are going – it is not stress-free and a long summer day's session will be exhausting.

Jigs are the other key weapon. They are too slow for searching a wide area but I use them

when I have pinned down a location to probe it accurately. They can take a bit of getting used to, though; with crankbaits I've found that if my boat partner is using the same lure as me and fishing it properly we'll catch more or less the same, but jigs are different: the angler's skill and experience really counts and I've had a drubbing or two from Michel, and have dished out rather more to others. The message here is that if your boat partner is catching and you're not then stop fishing and watch him until you work out what he is doing differently. At the start of one session in September 2004 I was being out-fished by Neil Roberts, so I watched him carefully and then slightly modified my technique to match his, with immediate success. I mentioned this to him, and he said that he thought he had been copying me! That shows what a difference barely noticeable variations in presentation can make. When you get it right jigging is a very fast way to take zander.

If I've got the day's technique sorted I expect to get fish as soon as the boat is in the correct

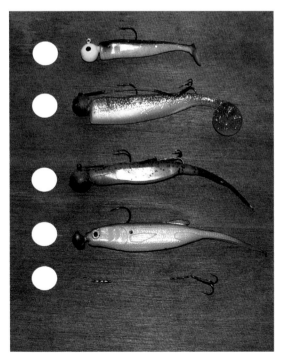

A selection of the jigs that Dave uses.

A selection of lure tackle.

position and I'll move off in less than ten minutes if there is no response; it usually only takes that long to catch all the fish in one spot. With an experienced jig angler like Tim Kelly aboard on a good day on the Severn I'd expect us to boat fifteen to twenty-five zander between us, with perhaps as many missed takes and lost fish; when Michel visited me in September 2004 one half-day session produced nineteen fish. We had takes in eleven out of the twelve swims we tried. Naturally Michel caught the majority (about twelve of them) – he's far too good for me when I have to control the boat as well. The size of the fish caught when jigging is generally quite small, and sometimes very small, but we get an occasional 8lb+ specimen and fish over 5lb are caught on most good sessions.

Tackle

For both techniques I use the same rod, one I put together myself (very roughly) using a St Croix

Avid AS56MF. This is a fast-tapered blank and is pretty universally used in Holland for jigging; it is great for trolling as well, although if I had to be really picky I'd prefer a slightly longer version for that. Whatever rod you choose for jigging it must have some backbone. Zander have a habit of grabbing a jig and just clamping on to it with their powerful jaw muscles, so you have to be able to dislodge that grip to set the hook. Lost fish are usually a result of an ineffective strike. I had one fish over 25ft in Holland come all the way to the surface before spitting the jig, and I've landed a few fish on the Avon that were not hooked but refused to let go of their prize. The quality of the rod, i.e. its taper and the amount of feedback it provides, will count a long way to your success with jigs.

A small fixed spool reel is the normal choice for both techniques, but a few anglers prefer a small low-profile multiplier. I recommend the fixed-spool choice. For me that means I can do a bit of casting with very light crankbaits or spinners for perch if the opportunity presents itself, but there is also the issue of overruns that are inconvenient and waste fishing time at best, and more importantly damage the fine braid required for good presentation. The most important thing is that the reel has no play when the anti-reverse is engaged; you jig with the anti-reverse on and any play that transmits through the rod will feel like a take and be immensely irritating. A smooth clutch is of course vital with this set-up; it has to be set just so that it doesn't give on the strike but runs freely if your zander is a big one or maybe turns into a lively double-figure pike.

From the bank I use 20lb test Power Pro or TUF braid, and on the boat I use 10lb b.s. Power-Pro braid. It took me a long time to convince myself that 10lb b.s. was strong enough; Michel finally converted me. He has since switched to 5lb test, which seems too fine to me, but I saw him land a low double pike with no problems on my last visit. I am convinced that for the best control of the lures either jigging or trolling the finer line is essential. When trolling, a finer line provides a far wider choice of lures that will hit the bottom in 15 to 20ft, which is where the majority of the zander can be caught, and when jigging a fine line means a more vertical presentation so you can fish more accurately to the echo sounder. With such fine line I've had no lost fish due to breakage, but losing lures is a constant expense. Being able to fish with a shorter line when trolling means you get closer control when fishing around snags and the more vertical line when jigging serves the same purpose, and this is some compensation. We do spend rather a lot of time most days, though, with the lure retriever. From the bank the lure retriever is of little use so stronger braid is the only way to reduce lure losses, but you never go home with as many as you brought with you.

A wire leader is essential for me because pike are present everywhere I fish. It does actually serve another purpose, though, and that is protecting the last foot of line that would otherwise take a hammering from the riverbed and from brushing against snags. In Holland they fish some waters that contain no pike, or virtually no pike, and they generally fish without a wire leader. There is a commercial element to this because big prizes (like Lund boats) are up for grabs in zander competitions, so if the successful anglers decide not to use wire then everyone follows. On my last Dutch trip (February 2004) Michel informed me that he was fishing without wire for all his jigging, even on the Maas with all its pike. On the third day he lost a small pike that bit through his line as he tried to hand-land it. This obviously changed his mind, and by some miracle of luck the next day using a wire leader he caught the same pike again and recovered the lost jig. I find it hard to believe that in the murky depths of the Severn or Avon (or anywhere else for that matter) a wire leader could make any difference to a fish biting a lead, steel and plastic jig.

A landing net is essential. Most zander can easily be hand-lifted from the water, but once over about 6lb I find it difficult to get a safe grip on them. Michel never takes a net for any of his fishing, and lost an estimated 22lb zander when trolling for pike. Be sure to have the net ready – a big zander does not always fight and you can

be fooled into thinking it is a small one until it breaks the surface. I lost a 15lb+ fish in 1997 because I thought I'd got another jack when trolling and didn't scream for the net until this monster rolled on the top. The single point of the Super Shad's belly treble just outside its mouth fell out as I watched; I can still see that zander if I close my eyes...

The echo sounder is the other indispensable piece of tackle for the boat. I see plenty of boats out without one, and I know why they don't catch as many fish as me. I watch the sonar screen continuously, so much so that when trolling my boat partner has to watch out for low-hanging branches and suchlike to avoid the occasional whack around the head. I've heard some anglers say that a cheap sounder will do, and a well-known tackle shop owner told me the same, too. I guess he's never used a good one. My zandering was immediately transformed when I swapped my old basic unit for a much more powerful Lowrance X87. I don't know, or need to know, the

A fish-finder is an absolute essential.

meaning of all the technical terms but 1500 watts peak-to-peak is the minimum power output you need. I fish to the sonar, using it to guide where I want my lures, and it does show fish. Several boat partners can testify to my saying: 'There's a zed!' followed by my getting a take and landing a fish. It takes a long time to get really familiar with a sounder but I reckon I am very good now, and that expertise catches me a lot of fish. If you look on the Lowrance website (and others) you will find useful guidance about how to get the best from the sounder: read it, understand it and practise it. It's a vital skill and could fill a chapter of any predator fishing book on its own.

Lures

Crankbaits first and trolling, your lure must stay in close contact with the riverbed. Your lure has to be within that foot or so of water above the bottom. It is impossible, given the variations in depth on the rivers, to guarantee that the lure is a fixed distance above the riverbed so the easy answer is to keep it touching the bottom. The rod tip should be constantly kicking as the lure bumps the bottom. Although some relatively shallow-diving crankbaits will dive a long way if you let enough line out, you lose control and find it difficult to time the lifts to get them over snags. The steeper the dive angles, the better the control you get. Lures in the 2 to 5ft range will catch most fish. I'll talk about bigger lures later.

A slim 'minnow' shape will catch more fish than a fatter-bodied one. This is nothing to do with the zander's preferences but down to simple mechanics; zander have relatively small mouths, so it is much more likely they will get a slimmer lure in their mouth and for that lure to get a good hook hold. I think this must be what led to the myth about zander taking lures from behind – if the zander hit the thinner tail of a lure it was much more likely to get hooked. Use slim lures and you hook the ones that hit the heads and middles as well, which is rather more than hit the tails. Take care of your leaders when trolling as some lures are very sensitive to kinks in

the leader. Some will be running at half depth but still giving a kicking sensation through the rod tip as they run off-line. Watch the line angle in the water and if it starts to get more acute you have a problem. The same thing can happen when your lure picks up debris. If you are not paying close attention you can go a long way with a mussel shell on the lure's belly treble, and I've never caught a fish like that.

Any slim lure that will hit the required depths will catch zander, or at least I haven't tried one that won't. I've obviously tried a lot of lures and have ended up with quite a selection but I will reduce that for the sake of simplicity to four that are the ones I use most often.

Manns Loudmouth 1 This is the easiest of all the crankbaits to use in terms of doing the depth and just staying in the fish's face at all speeds, though it picks up a lot of pike. I've broken a few of these on snags. Note that although this looks like a typical 'alphabet' crankbait from the side, it is narrow enough to be easily taken.

Cordell Wally Diver CD7 This is probably my most consistent catcher, though it is not as buoyant as the Loudmouth (some sink) and does not ride snags quite as well either. I've also used smaller sizes but they do not dive so deeply.

Rapala Deep Down Husky Jerk DHJ10 This is the hardest one to use for trolling as it is easy to 'lose' it, not knowing how deep it is running. It doesn't get as deep as the others, not much over 12ft. I use it because it is a very good catcher when depth allows, and it is good at low speed.

Storm Thundercrank 6cm and 9cm If these dived deeper I'd use them more as they are great catchers, and will catch plenty of perch and small pike as well. The 6cm gets down to about eleven feet, the 9cm a little more.

What matters about the choice of crankbait for trolling is not what it is called but what it does; reliable diving performance keeps the lure near to the zander for the maximum possible time and that is what counts. Trolling is demanding enough, and if you know your lure is in the slot that is one less thing to worry about. If you are trolling properly you are going to lose lures so take a few of each lure with you. I generally take four or five of each type, and I also keep spares at home so if I do drop a couple I am not waiting for a new delivery. If I want to try a new lure I always get a couple. The cost of lost lures is just part of the general expense. If time spent collecting live bait was taken into account then I suspect lures are not comparatively much more expensive.

Part of the lure choice equation is down to cost, and the cheaper they are, the better, as far as I'm concerned. The Rapala and Mann's ones are particularly expensive in the UK; I generally order from the USA or stock up on trips to Holland. It pays to keep an eye open for clearances, in most years suppliers like Cordell and Bomber will discontinue a colour or two and you can pick them up at a discount.

The same crankbaits can be used for casting, of course, but because retrieve speeds are slower you must have less buoyancy to get the lure deep enough, although bank swims are not as deep as the main trolling channel. Swim selection is very important; you are not going to be able to fish into even moderately deep water from the bank if you have a shallow-water ledge in front of you simply because the ledge will eat lures. This is what really cuts down on bank fishing opportunities – it is not the swim choice as much as the casting position that is the problem.

This can be quite demanding fishing, and perhaps difficult for inexperienced lure anglers, as it requires considerable understanding of what the lure is doing and careful control. Using something like a Rapala Deep Down Husky Jerk you must crank it down hard until it hits the riverbed, then pause, then pull it with the rod tip no more than a foot, take up the slack as you push the rod back ready for the next pull, and then pause. There are all sorts of difficulties – the flow can be too strong and the bottom can have too many snags – but if you can overcome the difficulties you can often catch a few. I have one swim where I can do this easily. It is only about six feet deep and has quite a good flow but the casting position from upstream makes lure control simpler than it would be from directly alongside it; there are

rather more swims where it is much more difficult.

To make life a little easier you might adjust the buoyancy of the lure a little. Usually a wire leader will sink so-called neutral-buoyancy lures but you might be able to use this to your advantage by having the leader resting on the riverbed with the lure just above it. But too strong a flow makes this at best frustrating and more usually impossible. In general you will want the lure to be just rising rather than just sinking when it pauses, and to increase buoyancy I use an adhesive-backed cork disc (these are sold in hardware shops in various sizes to put on the bottom of ornaments to prevent them scratching a polished surface), either on the lure or folded over the leader. You can of course add weight by either sticking on adhesive window lead or wrapping a little soldering wire around the hook shanks, or for very subtle adjustments changing the split rings for heavier versions, or adding a split ring or two to the hangers. A gram or two can make all the difference to your control.

Jigs are the simplest of lures, and the ones most often used wrongly. Many anglers see them as having no action so they insist on keeping them forever moving. For zander you need to slow down and get it under proper control. There are no brand names to highlight in respect of jigs used with a detachable soft plastic trailer. Any will do, provided they are of the right weight – between 15 and 30g, and with a sharp fine-wired round-bend hook with a small barb and in the size 2/0 (approx). Different shapes of lead head have been designed with different uses in mind, but for simplicity's sake I'd stick to a round head for casting, trolling or jigging; an 'Erie' shape is best used vertical jigging only.

Soft plastic trailers are available in a wonderful array of designs: paddle tails, curly tails, split tails, straight tails – and they all catch zander. There is also a fantastic range of beautiful and sometimes very realistic patterned finishes. Size matters, and anywhere between 2 and 6in is all right. I usually use trailers of around 4 to 5in. A reduction in size can often be the key to getting takes or turning tentative takes into proper hits, but most of the time (though certainly not invariably) missed takes are caused by the fish being too small to properly take the lure into its mouth. Other fish – especially small perch – can also cause frustrating missed takes; almost anything that swims will take a swipe at a jig from time to time.

Take care when threading the trailer onto the hook; you need to make most of the hook gape stand proud of the trailer's back. On a 5in trailer you will have over 3in of trailer without a hook so you need a stinger treble. Use a very sharp treble, and depending on the size of the trailer a size 6 or (more usually) 8 is about right, but different brands have different gapes. The preferred hook in Holland is the Gamakatsu model 13, widely available in the tackle shops over there but much more difficult to get hold of in the UK at present, and very expensive. I usually stock up on my Dutch trips and I certainly think that they are worth the money, even at UK prices. The stinger should be crimped on to 20lb 7-strand wire with a crimped loop at the other end that slips over the leader eye on the jig. You need a selection of stinger lengths that will suit different lengths of trailers. I usually use paddle, straight or split tails because the stinger suits them better. With a curl tail you either have a lot of tail behind the stinger, or you have to hook the curly bit and stop it wiggling, so defeating the object of using a curly tail. When a smaller trailer is required I might use a 2in curl tail without a stinger. Such a small curl tail helps avoid a blank session, although often it will be small perch and pike that you catch.

Other Lure Techniques

Occasionally zander will not be on the riverbed, but instead they will be suspended, perhaps 4ft down over 8ft. This is something that I have come across only recently and have only encountered a couple of times – probably because until I accidentally caught a few this way when pike fishing I had not tried it. It is obviously still 'work in progress' for me, and in a season or two I might have worked out when they are likely to be doing this. Neil Roberts tells me that he has caught some big zander in winter coloured-water conditions when fishing live baits 6ft deep over 14ft, so there is

The author with a lure-caught zander from the Ebro. Lures can work on any water.

certainly something to consider. The lure for this is a Rapala Husky Jerk HJ14. Just pull it down to mid-depth then give it a pull and leave it. While fishing last season, two fish from Wick (the same spot where I caught my first zander, it's still a very good swim) hit the lure after it had been hanging for over five seconds. So don't rush it. They were nice fish – about 4lb and 6lb – and maybe only fairly big zander behave in this way, because of the danger from pike or bird predation while swimming at that level.

Another phenomenon that I have experienced just a few times is finding zander hiding in lily pad beds on the Avon. I'm not sure how often this happens or how many fish are involved, but I've caught a handful of smallish fish when jigging through pads (for pike) over about six feet of water. The few incidents have always been on bright days in August, which leads me to suspect that it is connected to high water temperature or strong light and low summer flows.

I have used a variety of bottom bouncer type systems to try to keep lures close to the river-bed whilst protecting them from snagging. I have caught some zander with these, including a wonderful seven fish (3 to 4lb size) in twenty minutes. The different set-ups for this, and the reasons why each have their uses, are beyond the scope of this overview of lure techniques; they do have some useful applications, especially for the bank angler, but as my boat handling skills have increased I have found less use for them when afloat.

In general, zander complete their spawning late in May and are very aggressive in defending their nests for a while afterwards, and although they have completed their parental duties by the start of the river season on 16 June they still retain much of their aggression. This can lead to some surprise catches, with quite modest zander hitting some very big and unlikely lures; sadly it doesn't last beyond the first week of July but it can provide some amusement. The lure fishing during the first fortnight of the season is as good as it gets, though – it's the zander equivalent of the trout angler's 'duffers' fortnight'. September can also be very good.

Big Zander

The small lure techniques listed above produce a lot of zander, the vast majority of which are under 4lb in weight. As a rough guide, for every pound in weight size increase, we catch a third less, so for every thirty 1lb fish we catch twenty 2lb fish, and for every twenty 2lb fish we get fourteen 3lb fish, and so on. Fish above 7lb are comparatively scarce, and although I've accumulated a few 8lb and 9lb fish over the last few years I have not seen a double with these techniques.

I know that big zander will take small lures from my Dutch experience. One of Michel's friends had a 14lb+ fish on a small jig, and I've seen a Dutch video where a 20lb+ zander was landed, again on a regular jig. But it hasn't happened to me over here; in several hundred fish over the past seasons I've not cracked the double barrier with these 'numbers' techniques, despite having a lot of fun.

In November 2004 I was pike fishing near Tewkesbury when my boat partner, Seb Shelton, was suddenly into a good fish, fighting well and obviously a double. Just before it surfaced I realized it was a big zander, and it weighed 14lb 6oz, which was quite stunning. We were trolling with pike-sized lures. As the so-called 'zander lure expert' I naturally took a bit of stick about this fish but luckily it did not take long for me to catch my own. On 31 January 2005 near Upton-On-Severn

Dave Pugh with a stunning lure-caught floodwater zander in excess of 15lb.

my turn came. It hit the lure in around ten feet of water and came to the surface immediately, where we instantly saw it was a big zander. This one weighed 15lb 7oz. In the 2004/05 season I had another three doubles at 16lb 11oz, 11lb 7oz and 10lb, while Seb, on one of his rare Severn visits, had another at 10lb 5oz. I've yet to get a double from the Avon, but I fish it less often and very seldom use big lures.

Obviously these are good fish, but considering the amount of time I spend out on the river using similar lures and techniques they are not

Lures can work on the smallest or the biggest of waters. The author on the hunt for zander at Grafham Water.

exactly regular captures. It is difficult to build much of a picture up with just these six fish, but taking into account rather more fish in the 8lb+ category that have fallen to pike-sized lures there are a few pointers that might help make them a less irregular capture.

The first consideration, as always, is location. The vast majority of the swims that produce numbers of small fish to small lure techniques are not worth looking at, unless they have some form for 6lb+ specimens. Small zander have different requirements as regards prey size for one thing, and they are also not keen on sharing their homes with double-figure pike. The big zander have nearly all come from good pike areas, not exactly the same spots as the pike but nearby. The key in terms of the river profile is to find a sloping drop-off, not so steep that it would be a good pike feature (although it might be steeper nearby) in the depth range of around ten to fifteen feet. Lots of work with the sonar is required to learn where these areas are, and they are not at a fixed distance from the bank either. Also note that big zander are not so fixated with depth, so they can be quite high up on that slope.

All of the doubles I caught came on days when the pike were difficult, although we've had quite a few 8lb and 9lb samples (poor James Ashworth has had 9lb14oz and 9lb15oz zander) on good pike days. Water clarity and light levels must be important but it is very difficult to work out sometimes what the fish are seeing. Seb's 14lb 6oz came under average clarity (about eighteen inches) and moderate light from around twelve feet depth, my 15lb 7oz came in about a foot of visibility on a very stormy day, and my 16lb 11oz came in Sep-

A hugely impressive shot of a Grafham 14lb 14oz fish to Alan Ward.

tember when local rain had dirtied the water so there was barely six inches of clarity from about ten feet and light levels that had been good in the morning had fallen as cloud moved in.

Although I'm sure we are going to catch more doubles over the coming seasons I would not like to predict when. I certainly do not go out expecting to catch one, and I think anyone expecting to, on any given day, is misguided. You need persistence and some luck. Having said that, I would not be at all surprised if the next record zander came out on a lure. Although far more anglers use fish baits than lures for their zandering I suspect many bait anglers reduce their chances of catching big ones by using baits that are too small, simply because they get too many missed takes (from smaller zander) on larger baits. Big lures, with fine-wired hooks, are far more effective hookers than big baits. Many anglers who have bait fished on the Severn for pike with live baits in the 8 to 10in range have caught a few good zander, and missed rather more small ones.

For the future I plan to explore more of the river and get away from heavily fished areas. I've

not tried night fishing with lures but I'm sure some of the apparent contradiction between lure and bait fishing results are down to the difference between daytime and nighttime behaviour. And finally, a bit of speculation – I always joke that I am fishing for a 20lb zander every time I go out, and there may be one in there somewhere.

There is little I can add to Dave's experienced commentary except to reiterate that if you do plan to mount a lure campaign for zander be aware that it can be an expensive game. Parts of the Severn will snag everything, and if you are not hitting bottom you are not where the zander are for most of the time. In addition I have realized that if I take the boat out equipped with both bait and lure equipment I end up fishing neither effectively, so for most of the last few seasons I have fished mainly lures. In 2004/05 I caught a lot of zander on lures as I continued to learn, the best of which was a fish of 8lb 14oz. Surprise fish can come to anyone, an example being my good friend Steve Sault who was pike fishing using Bulldawgs. First cast caught a 23lb pike and the next cast a double-figure zander on a Dawg.

10 THE SEA BAIT DEBATE

Denis Moules

If you asked most serious zander anglers their opinion of sea baits I think most would reply that they were okay for pike, but not really any good for zander. This is something I agree with. In all the time that I have fished the Fens, for both pike and zander, I have never caught a zander on a sea bait of any type. Going further than that, I have seen only two with my own eyes, one on a herring from the Cam, and the other from the Sixteen Foot Drain.

That these two venues are the only ones from which I have seen them caught is not really as much of a surprise as you may think. There seems to be an increase in the number of zander that are caught on dead sea baits, interestingly mostly on those drains where there are good heads of pike and pike anglers. Why this should be so is difficult to say. However, it could just be that familiarity with sea baits has made the zander look upon them as an easy, free meal, particularly when food may be scarce.

As I have no experience myself of catching zander on dead sea baits my good friend Denis Moules has written this chapter, and has drawn not only on his own experience, but also on that of other anglers from his large circle of friends that have caught zander on sea baits.

The Sixteen Foot Drain produces a number of zander to sea baits, but this ten-pounder preferred roach.

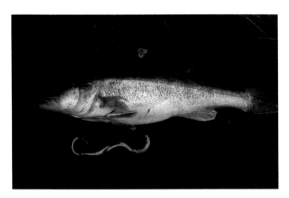

There are no doubts as to what this zander preferred.

A selection of sea deads.

What is Sea Bait?

Sea bait, for the purpose of this article, is fish that live in salt water and are used by predator anglers in fresh and still waters to catch predatory fish. These fish include mackerel, herring, sardine, pilchard, sprat, garfish, sand eel, launce, and other marine species.

I also categorize smelt as sea bait. I am well aware that others may have a different view on this as smelt are sometimes found in fresh water. This is usually confined to areas around sluices that link fresh to tidal water. They will swim into fresh water when the sluice is open, but so do flounder and dabs, and I have never heard them described as anything other than sea fish. In tidal rivers such as the Hundred Foot Drain smelt are found as far inland as Brownshill Staunch at Over, Cambridgeshire. This is the point where the tidal water ends. I have never known of smelt to venture too far inland in fresh water (we don't appear to have them at Cambridge). So I rest my case.

Introduction

The zander has always been an enigmatic and mysterious fish with no set behavioural pattern. Soon after its introduction and subsequent spread across the Fens it became a predictable problem. Fish stocks were decimated as it quickly colonized. In recent years it appears to have changed

its habits, feeding nocturnally, taking an assortment of lures during the daytime and taking sea bait. In general it now avoids anglers. Big zander, at the time of writing, are decidedly rare, with very few of specimen size being reported.

The debate over whether sea bait works or not has only cropped up in the last few years. One or two predator anglers say it does work now and again. Some are even convinced it is a viable option, often fishing sea bait intended for zander on one or two rods. Many specialist zander anglers say it doesn't work. A specialist zander angler, however, will know his job and uses whatever means are necessary. Most zander specialists I know do not fish sea bait on any of their rods and therefore they have no experience of catching zander on sea bait.

So who is right? Basically everyone appears to be is saying the same thing – yes, zander can be caught on sea bait, but not consistently and only on certain waters and in certain conditions. To the best of my knowledge no top-50 zander has been taken on sea bait.

Very little has been written on the subject. *Zander*, by Neville Fickling and Barrie Rickards, stated, 'Several big zander have been taken on sea bait, but if you use them for zander you are in for a long wait'. There is no mention of the captors or weight of fish. Steve Younger, in his book *Fenland Zander*, mentions that he is only aware of a few

The Middle Level Main Drain, not a water where I would use sea baits, in common with every other zander water.

Denis Moules with a land drain caught zander taken on mackerel.

accidental captures on herring and smelt by pike anglers. He was not aware of anyone who had regularly caught zander on them, and at the time of his writing (1996) had caught none himself. Steve considered that anyone fishing for zander with sea bait was 'stacking the odds against yourself'.

I have read many articles in magazines and angling publications and I cannot recall anyone mentioning the topic until recently. During the 1980s I caught no zander whatsoever on sea bait, despite the fact I fished most of the drains and rivers consistently – an average 1½ days a week from October to March each season. Pike anglers who I associated and fished with never mentioned catching zander on sea fish. It was always the roach or eel that was taken. Come to mention it, few people mentioned catching zander on lures. If one was caught it was on a Silver Toby. Nowadays anglers specifically target zander with lures. Dave Gaunt – that hugely successful zander fisherman – seems to have perfected the art. So what has changed in relation to sea baits? Is it the zander or the environment it lives in?

In the 1970s and 1980s there were a lot more zander about. In fact when they first arrived in

some waters, they were in abundance, compared to food fish. Why didn't they take the sea bait then? And if they did, why did no one talk about it? Even during the infamous 'cull' days for predators in 1980–81, when the pike/zander ratio to other species was huge, zander were not being caught on sea fish

I have no doubt that zander were eating sea fish, or at least those species that reside in the Tidal Great Ouse and Hundred Foot Drain, from the moment they first arrived following their 'escape' from the Relief Channel where they were first introduced. This would be around 1966–67 and was well described by Cliff Cawkwell and John McAngus in a paper written in 1976, and published in *Angler's Mail*.

I appreciate that freshwater fish, namely roach and bream, would also have escaped with them, but would a hungry zander be able to differentiate between a small dab or flounder and a freshwater fish in the murky, muddy tidal water? I doubt it – a hungry zander will eat almost anything.

From the late 1980s to the early 1990s the zander population appeared to have fallen on many Fenland waters, and this coincided with

The camera never lies – Ian Moules with a zander caught on mackerel.

the apparent readiness for zander to take sea bait. Some waters, such as the Middle Level, Great Ouse and Cut Off Channel, appeared to hold their own with zander stocks, hence the number of specimen zander reported from these waters. These are healthy Fenland waters when you compare them with those that are subject to environmental hazards, such as the Delph and Old Bedford. Pollution on these waters is regular and bad enough to be a severe problem to the anglers that fish there.

The zander is a very vulnerable species and is often the first to perish in adverse conditions. So why have zander in recent years seemed to favour sea bait, despite being fewer in numbers? I can only recollect my own experiences and others who have fished the Fenland area during the time zander have been with us.

My Experience with Sea Bait

I have fished the Cambridgeshire and Norfolk Fens since I was a small boy, and have rarely fished elsewhere. I have seen pike anglers come and go, likewise zander anglers, some good, some bad.

I am first and foremost a pike fisherman. I have captured 20s from most of the Fenland waters. Occasionally I have fished seriously and specifically for zander for short periods of time. At the time of writing, I'm having a few 'Z' days, and when conditions are comfortable a 24-hour session is completed with my son Ian.

Most of my zander have been captured while pike fishing. My record for zander is somewhat modest as a result, with six doubles to 14lb 12oz. But I have taken more than seventy at over 8lb,

Another sea bait caught zander.

thirty-eight of which were taken in February/ March 1986 from the Old Bedford, 2½ miles south of Salter's Lode. I presume that several of these were recaptures. I have never been one to follow the crowd, hence I did not fish the Middle Level in its heyday and similar prolific waters. I like to find my own fish.

In the late 1960s through to the 1990s few anglers mentioned catching zander on sea fish baits. Some stated that zander would not take them under any circumstances. I believed them, as I had caught none either. I first captured zander on sea fish in the 1992–93 season. I was fishing a land drain deep into the heart of Fenland. This drain was pumped into a main river in winter and water was let in from the main river in summer for irrigation. It held large stocks of most freshwater species and was always well coloured. A farmer friend, Trevor, informed me zander were present in the Drain in numbers – 'Big ones,' he said. He went on to tell me about a gypsy worker who had set a deadline in the drain baited with lob worms. He was hoping to catch an eel for his supper. On retrieving the line the following morning, the young traveller was in for a shock. Yes, he had caught an eel, but a large zander had, in turn, taken the eel and was well-hooked in the throat. Trevor measured out the full length of the fish on his arm. It was a big one. The travellers were well fed that night.

I began to fish the drain, starting with a double on eel sections, and caught several nine-pounders. I caught a few pike too from this small water – its winter depth is only 2ft 6in. There were some good doubles too. I began to use sea bait to target pike, namely sardine, herring and mackerel. I assumed the near zero temperatures would render the zander semi-dormant, as they appeared to be in the Main Drains. The change of bait made no difference whatsoever and zander to 9lb 14oz took my sea bait regularly. On certain days I expected to catch zander on sea bait. Fishing companions. Andrew Smith and Ian Jakes fared likewise. Barrie Rickards had a brace of eights on half mackerel on a daytime autumn visit with me. The sport came to an abrupt end when a diesel spillage entered

the drain and wiped out the zander. The pike survived and grew on to big 20's, 27½lb being my best. To my knowledge no other predator anglers were regularly fishing the water. Discarded bait and the zander taking a liking to it did not come into play. No pre-baiting was taking place. Why the zander took sea fish in this tiny water was a mystery to me. I put it down at the time to its being a 'one-off water' – its size, water colour and possibly pike competition all contributing. I had never confronted such circumstances before.

In January 2002 I was fishing an area of the Ramsey Forty Foot with son Ian and my friend Michael Bradford. The dawn start had revealed little in the way of sport and we were slowly leap-frogging along the drain. Suddenly the action started. Ian landed a 17lb 14oz pike, and a pack of zander moved in. It was apparent they were in a feeding frenzy. Baits were being taken in all directions and two or three were landed on half mackerel and sardines before the sport came to an abrupt end. Since that day I have never caught another there on sea bait, despite several visits to the area.

I have fished the River Cam since 1970, the middle reaches being only a five-minute drive from my home. Zander in numbers were in the river from 1974. I have fished it regularly for pike with friends, but never caught zander on sea bait

A more conventional bait caught this fish for Denis, and a real beast at 14lb.

Michael Bradford with an 8lb zander caught on smelt.

Even on a heavily fished stretch of the Cut Off Channel that sees plenty of pike baits and captures, this 14lb fish caught by Cheryl Tomline still preferred roach.

until the 2003/04 season, despite the sea fish being my most-used bait. In November 2003 I was with Michael Bradford. The river was running and coloured. Debris was coming down, covering most of the surface, making float fishing difficult. Michael dispensed with his float and fished one rod only with popped up smelt, beach-caster style on an 'optonic'. An 8lb 9oz zander obliged.

A few weeks later the Cam was again fining down after a flood, coloured with a strong flow and overcast with a strong westerly wind. These are the conditions I love. 'You don't go fishing – you are called,' David Fogg, a very successful Fenland piker, once told me, and how right he was. I gave up my usual Sunday pint and went zandering. Out went a live roach, a dead roach and an eel section – for zander – and my fourth rod, in case a pike was on the move, was baited with sardine.

After an hour or so, I cut off the sardine's head and recast. An oily slick moved downstream. Around 2.30pm the sardine was rapidly on the move downstream. A firm strike hooked the fish, which bumped and boiled in typical zander fashion. The fish, duly landed, was, at 10lb 9oz, my largest zander ever from the Cam.

Why did it take the sardine when freshwater bait was close by? Had the coloured water that was on the move disoriented it, or had the roach that normally shoaled on the gravel bed I was fishing dispersed, leaving my sardine with its scent trail an attractive option? I will never know. She was certainly well fed, with a fat belly.

Later that season Michael Bradford and I decided to leapfrog a stretch of the Cam in the Middle Reaches that rarely sees an angler. After a long walk we wiped the cow dung off our boots, having taken what should have been a short-cut through Cyril West's cow sheds. We began to leapfrog with the flow towards Upware. It was a bitterly cold day but conditions were good – a brisk wind from the north-west blew in our faces, the water was coloured and running off nicely but ripple free, owing to the wind's position. Midday came, no runs, but after several moves downstream I eventually had a run on a popped up smelt for a 7lb 2oz zander. This turned out

to be the only run of the day. Since then I have captured no more Cam zander on sea bait; and come to that I've had none anywhere else either.

If there is one Fenland water that I would expect to catch zander on sea bait, it is the tidal Hundred Foot Drain, between Earith and Mepal. I have fished this water regularly since 1975 and have never taken one on sea bait, but have taken several on freshwater fish and eel.

So there it is. About twenty-five zander caught on sea bait since 1992, an average of fewer than two a season, from three different waters. Although all the zander were over 7lb I do not think it is a convincing argument to persuade anglers to use the method expecting instant success.

Others' Experience with Sea Bait

It is obvious that one man and a few friends who fish with him will not give a true picture of what is going on in the whole of Fenland with regard to zander and sea bait. Although I know and fish with a lot of honest and well-respected predator anglers, I have not personally visited some Fenland waters for years, and with the sheer mileage of water available my personal experiences have to be taken at face value. It is worth, therefore, recording the experiences of some of my associates who I know are successful and regular anglers elsewhere in the catchments. It is also important to consider whether zander have been captured when pike fishing or by design – the captor having formed an opinion that using sea bait is an effective method to target zander.

I asked Neville Fickling to expand on his comments in his book on zander. He only knows of three other well-known anglers who have captured zander on sea bait, but only three of the fish were up to 10lb. These were very early captures, as his book was first published in 1979.

John McAngus was bailiff for the Great Ouse River Authority, Fenland area during the 1970s. He has witnessed many zander captures but cannot ever recall one coming to sea bait whilst he was in office. John's 'beat' did not cover the Relief or the Cut Off Channels and sadly the

Ian Moules with a 14lb + fish caught on conventional baits.

Cheryl Tomline with part of a four doubles in a day catch of zander, a feat I would love to emulate.

bailiffs of these waters, Cliff Cawkwell and Douglas Yates, have passed away.

The very highly respected Bill Chillingworth, former record holder with a 15lb 5oz from the Relief Channel in February 1971, has noticed a remarkable change in zander feeding habits on the Cut Off Channel during the last ten to twelve years. Bill states that he has captured twelve to fourteen zander in all on sardine and mackerel, with fish to 12lb. Most of Bill's fish are between 7 and 8lb, with nothing less than 5lb. Bill wondered whether it is pre-baiting with sea fish that has switched them over. Bill is confident that at times a small sardine will out-fish freshwater dead bait, and he quite happily fishes sardine for zander on his dead bait rods. Bill never uses smelt.

Steve Rodwell, another Cut Off Channel expert, has captured five doubles on smelt, up to 12lb, and Dave Horton, who was a frequent visitor to the Rodwell network of waters, has taken zander of 13lb and 10lb on smelt, an eight-pounder on sardine and two six-pounders on herring.

Moving over to the Western area, March's John Watson captured a 10lb+ zander on half a mackerel, from the Old River Nene ten years ago. He has also taken six of between 5 and 6lb on smelt. As a matter of interest, John has also taken a double-figure zander on three lobworms.

Likewise, Alan Ward and Paul Wilton have had a few. Alan took his first in 1994 to smelt, 13lb 9oz from the Old Bedford, and Paul captured the same fish two weeks later, also to smelt. Alan has taken a further double to smelt from the Delph in 2003/04. Paul has taken a brace of 11lb and 9lb from the Middle Level in the same session on ½ mackerel and a further two of 9lb from the Relief Channel on the same bait.

My friends Ian and Cheryl Tomline have found that the zander on the Old River Nene like smelt, having taken several around 5 to 7lb in recent years. Cheryl has also taken two doubles of 12lb 3oz on pilchard and 10lb 3oz on smelt from the Cut Off Channel at Black Dyke Outfall, backed by a 9lb on sardine.

Jamie Groom has taken ten zander to 9lb on smelt from the Old River Nene in recent seasons, and one of 7lb on a huge ½ mackerel. Jamie has also captured an 8lb 7oz zander on sand eel from this water. The River Ouse zander at Wyboston have also responded to his sea bait, with 9lb to herring, 5lb 12oz on sprat and 7lb to sand eel. Cheryl and Jamie are quick to admit they were pike fishing.

The 'stars', however, have to be my friends Andrew Blazey and Richard Wesley, fishing on the Great Ouse since 1997. Andy has taken over thirty zander on sea fish to 11lb 8oz, including four doubles. All were 6lb+. Richard has taken over twenty, including two doubles and five over 9lb. These two anglers target zander, fishing three rods, two on live bait and a 'sleeper' rod with a herring bait. Herrings are fresh, not blast-frozen ones. They do not fish many zander sessions a season, preferring to pike fish, which puts their captures in perspective.

There are many fellow predator anglers I could have given a mention to, but the story appears the same amongst all those I have spoken to. Yes, a few zander have been captured on sea bait, usually sizeable ones after several years of fishing – which is much like myself.

Personally, I shall be sticking with these!

Conclusion

Drawing on my own and others' experiences I have summarized the main points relating to catching zander on sea bait:

1. Zander taking sea bait is a fairly recent phenomenon (since late 1980s).
2. Zander will take sea bait occasionally on most Fenland waters.
3. Zander captured on sea bait are usually sizeable, i.e. between 7 and 14lb.
4. Zander seem to prefer sea bait in coloured, running water.
5. A pack of zander in a feeding frenzy are more likely to take sea bait than solitary fish.
6. Don't expect to catch many zander on sea bait.
7. Few specialist zander anglers fish with sea bait.
8. Sprats would appear to be the least successful of regularly used sea bait, but zander have occasionally been caught by friends using them as wobbled dead bait.

11 SOMETIMES EVERYTHING GOES WRONG: ON THE LIGHTER SIDE

Throughout this book, and in most other angling books, you will have read about how to get things right and catch consistently. However, what you will not have read about are the times when it all goes wrong, and when all the best-laid plans come crashing down around the 'expert's' ears. Well, read on.

Adventures Afloat

Most keen predator anglers will at some stage in their fishing career have ventured out onto the water in some kind of vessel. Well I am no exception, and I have been afloat on many different craft, of varying degrees of water worthiness.

This story, though, centres around one particular vessel, a little fibreglass dinghy that Ollie, a friend, owns and which I christened, without affection, 'washing-up tub'. It acquired such a label because it shared with its namesake the same characteristics of stability. However, this was all ahead of us one mild November day as I waited on the banks of Roswell Pits for Ollie to dock in the 'tub' to ferry me over to Rat Island in the middle of the lake, where Ollie, Ashley, Winky and I were planning to do a four-day session.

Eventually a ship approached out of the rapidly failing light with Ollie paddling away. Standing as I was on a railway sleeper higher than the water the boat looked awfully small, especially as we had some more equipment to load into it, including a large bag of apples that I had brought from the market stall that I worked on at that time. As Ollie pulled into the side he uttered the fateful words 'Don't try and get aboard until I am ready.' Now unfortunately I only heard the last part of that statement, and tried to quickly step

into the middle of the boat. Alas my aim wasn't good and instead of landing in the boat, I stepped straight onto the side, off the boat and into the water. As I sunk into the water up to my waist, I looked around to expect to see Ollie laughing at me, but instead all I saw was the upturned hull of the boat and no sign of Ollie. I lifted up the hull and there was Ollie, standing in the water but bent over at the waist with the 'washing-up tub' on top of him.

The next part of the conversation was completely unrepeatable, as you can imagine. I have to say that I couldn't help but see the funny side, especially as a bedraggled-looking Ollie got more and more irate, whilst all around him bobbed apples and various items of tackle and food. We did eventually get all the equipment back into the boat, and ourselves to the island. The funniest part of the clean-up operation was the discovery that Ollie wasn't wet above the waist, as he had actually done a perfect somersault and landed in the still-seated position, only minus the boat. He hadn't even got the tobacco in his chest pocket wet!

Scaling Everest

This adventure also takes place at Roswell Pits, which is pretty unsurprising really, as a lot of my formative zander angling was done there.

Roswell itself is a clay pit dug into a valley of sorts, and as such has banks that are a lot higher than the water level. To fish you have to come down steps or steep banks to access the water comfortably. One side of the lakes in particular is worse than the others, in that there is a good difference in height between the top of the bank and

Safer climes, and no mountaineering needed this time.

the water's edge. It is also one of the better areas of the lake, in that it allows a reasonably easy cast to the margins of one of the several islands that are present.

It was here that Ashley, Ollie and I had chosen to spend our weekend, and had enjoyed a very good one taking several zander and a few pike, as well as a bonus 2lb rudd that I caught whilst catching bait. However, the Saturday night had been a real monsoon that had seen us all confined to our bivvies pretty much all night. As we all embarked upon the worst part of all angling, packing up, we didn't realize just how bad things were about to get.

I cannot recall who first attempted to climb back up the steep bank behind us, but knowing how slow Ollie is at doing everything I doubt it was him. I do recall that they stumbled upon a problem, which was that with any degree of extra loading it was impossible to get any traction at all, and they just slid straight back down the bank, the night's rain having turned the clay bank into a slippery slope that we had to try to scale with three people's weekend fishing kit.

Getting round this problem involved a large degree of thought, and even more sweating, swearing and sliding. To pull the equipment up

Add one eel and this is all you get left.

we had to form a human chain, with myself at the top and Ashley and Ollie below me, clinging on to small bushes, shrubs, basically anything that would provide us just a bit of grip. That whole mountaineering exercise took us over two hours to complete, and on more than one occasion one member of the expedition would suddenly arrive at the man below as purchase was lost. I never fished that bank again!

Ouse Sorry Now?

These two stories both centre on a small stretch of the River Ouse running through the town centre at Ely, and which has played a large part in my zandering throughout my lifetime.

The first one involves (yet again) Ollie, and unfortunately he takes the brunt of the disaster once more. If it seems like Ollie has a higher than average degree of disasters than any other person you have met, that's almost certainly because he has. In addition to the previous exploits that I mentioned earlier, I have also seen Ollie almost set fire to himself, Ashley's bivvy and half of France whilst trying to fill a petrol stove by candlelight, amongst many, many other calamities.

This one, though, took some beating from my point of view, and had me in tears for many days afterwards. We were, unusually, bivvied up for the night between the railway and high bridges through Ely and were having something of a quiet night, with neither the local drunks nor

Brewing up on the Ouse. Watch out for slugs!

the zander bothering us. As was our want at the time, we stayed up for the greater part of the night putting the world to rights and drinking copious amounts of tea. Some time in the early hours I had lost the toss for who was to make the next cuppa and, with the habit so deeply ingrained, I managed to complete the task without any artificial light. We sat talking and laughing some more whilst contemplating the latest mug of tea, and as was usual I had long ago finished mine whilst Ollie was taking his time. In fact I was already reminding him of the fact that he was next on the kettle as he drained his mug, only to start coughing and retching, before coughing something up onto the grass. On inspection in the head-torch that something turned out to be a huge, great, black slug. Ollie by this time was in the bushes being violently ill and cursing me with all the names that he could think of, for not checking the cup.

It's a check that I perform even to this day.

For a change Ollie wasn't involved in this next story, in fact the victim of this incident wasn't even an angler but instead one of the many boaters, or 'weekend admirals' as we prefer to call them.

Richard and I were fishing close to the railway bridge and, as the day passed by, a boater pulled up just to my right. As he tied the boat to a stake that he had thoughtfully hammered into the bank he suddenly pulled up, clutching at his right hand with his left. He then proceeded to walk towards us and came up to me.

'Have you got anything to remove this?' he asked, whilst simultaneously revealing a large set of trebles that were now thoroughly embedded into his hand. 'Yes I have, mate,' I replied, 'but it will hurt!' Strangely, for some reason the unfortunate boater was happy for me to perform amateur surgery with only a pair of forceps, and so I clamped them on and got him to brace his arm with the other one. The cry of pain that left that guy's lips as I began to pull was pretty impressive, I have to say. Less impressive was the fact that, in his agony, he couldn't brace the arm enough, and my tugs were only causing pain without threatening to remove the hooks. A new plan was needed.

Summoning Richard to join us, I got Richard to stand behind the chap whilst I pulled on the offending trebles. Again the cries from the hooked boater were outstanding, whilst my Dr Kildare impression was hampered somewhat by the fact that all I could see was Richard crying with laughter behind him. However, there was an audible tearing sound, followed by me almost falling backwards as the hooks at last came free. The poor man by now was pretty much devoid of colour, whilst Richard was turned away, bent double with mirth. The weekend admiral even thanked me profusely.

Enjoying the Wildlife

Whoever said that there's more to fishing than catching fish couldn't have been more right. In my time spent angling I have been privileged to see some wonderful sights involving our native wildlife. In my time I have seen hobbies, merlin, harriers, kites and peregrines amongst our rare birds of prey, as well as otters, deer and other mammals swimming in rivers and drains around the Fens.

However, not all wildlife is so welcome. My main protagonists seem to be swans. Now, most people love swans but to my mind they are the single most stupid creatures that inhabits our waterways. I have broken a rod thanks to swans, where my patience finally snapped when for the millionth time that night the swans had swum through my lines on the Ouse, only this time they had also managed to wrap the line around a stand of reeds. I was unaware of this fact as I savagely thrashed the rod up to clear the line, only for it to snap with a sound like a gunshot as it broke at the spigot.

On another occasion I was sitting back enjoying a mild winter's day fishing from a slightly high bank opposite Roswell Pits. As the day slipped by I was aware of the large number of swans on the river, and the fact that one cob swan was taking great exception to these interlopers.

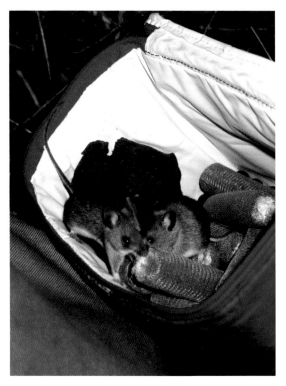

Some wildlife I enjoy. Mice are fine, swans less so.

Eventually his patience snapped and he strove to drive these newcomers from his territory. The three young swans that the cob was chasing came hurtling round the bend to my right in semi-airborne state, but worst of all within a yard or two of the bank, and my lines. Basically I had no chance and all three rods were wiped out simultaneously amongst a howling of delkims, the hissing of swans and the world's worst tangle.

Swans, I hates 'em!

A Man's Best Friend

There is a multitude of tales that I could tell about my late fishing dog, Merlin. In his time he developed a personality and reputation of his own to the extent where if he wasn't with me, most people would ask as to his whereabouts and we were viewed very much as a partnership, one which was sadly ended all too early.

Man's best friend indeed…Merlin soon deserted the sinking ship.

My favourite mishap wasn't really his fault, for once, but he did display a scant disregard for his master's predicament. Once again the scene was Roswell, and once again there was a boat involved, a completely jinxed vessel that I bought, did up (including a natty camouflage paint job) and then sold after a series of disasters befell me whilst afloat in it, this one being the final straw.

I had decided to do a night over on the island in the middle of the pit, an island that could at a squeeze hold two anglers. The size, though, wasn't an issue that night as there was only myself and Merlin aboard the boat, plus a mountain of angling equipment for an overnight session, planned to involve a bit of boat angling the next day. The boat was quickly loaded and I got in whilst Merlin, in the manner of all springer spaniels, leapt aboard with gusto. The short journey to the island was undertaken, and we pulled up alongside the pallet platform used for landing. I stepped off the boat and went straight through a very rotten pallet. I was now left in the precarious position of having one foot right through a rotten wooden pallet, the other still in the boat. For a

Just occasionally it does go right and a fish like this twelve-pounder gets caught.

Sometimes I manage to avoid the disasters and catch zander.

few moments stalemate ensued as I tried to free my leg, but with no purchase I wasn't moving anywhere fast. Merlin then chose this moment to use me as a bridge to gain access to the island.

There was only one way that I was getting out of the pallet, and that was to push free with my other leg, but there lay more difficulties, as I was standing on the very front of the boat, and by pressing down hard with that foot I would push the bows under the water. It soon became apparent that I would have to take that path. Trying to be as quick as possible I thrust myself forward, at which point the boat promptly three-quarters filled with water and was almost sunk completely. I managed to drag my bedchair, rucksack, etc. out

of the water with as little water ingress as I could manage. However, my brand new Coleman double burner was now perched on the stern of the boat, and my attempts at emptying the boat of water were making it wobble in a scene reminiscent of the ending of *The Italian Job* where the bus hangs over the edge of the mountain road, before Michael Caine says the immortal words 'Listen, lads, I have a plan.' Well so did I, only in my case it ended up with the Coleman hanging tantalizingly out of reach before sliding into the deep.

There is a happy ending in that, after many casts, I finally managed to retrieve the stove with the aid of a jerkbait rod and a bulldawg lure. The boat was sold by the end of the week.

12 EBRO ZANDER – ENGLISH-STYLE

'Fancy coming over to the Ebro and having a go for the zander?' This was the offer extended to me by Martin Walker from Catfish Capers; well, it would have been rude to turn that kind of offer down, wouldn't it? So as everybody else was soothing their bank accounts from the Christmas excess, I boarded a plane from Stanstead, heading for Zaragoza in Spain and bound for the River Ebro.

This first visit was in the winter of 2006 and from that moment on a love affair with Spain and the zander of the mighty River Ebro of the north of the country has dragged me back time after time.

The Ebro has drawn many English anglers to its banks, predominantly for the large head of big catfish that the river holds. However, few, it seems, have targeted the numerous zander that the river also holds. Like our zander, the fish of the Ebro were introduced into the river as a non-native, the common story being that they were put in, along with the cats and bleak, as an experiment by a German fisheries scientist. If the experiment was to see if the fish would prosper, then they most certainly have, now being prolific throughout the river.

For my trip we were concentrating on the area around the Catfish Capers base in Caspe. Going with an established tour company is, in my opinion, the way to go, as all the equipment that

With scenery like this it would have been rude not to accept Martin Walker's offer of a trip to the Ebro.

you need is supplied. This becomes all the more important when you consider the restrictions imposed by some of the low-cost airlines. Ryanair, for instance (the only carrier into Zaragoza), now has a 15kg limit on hold luggage. As this was somewhat of an exploratory trip, I took a few items of tackle with me, and getting all of this, plus clothes and essentials, under 15kg became very difficult. Certainly some can be spread over the hand luggage, but as there are further restrictions on the size of that, the reality is that they are not spread very much.

The added advantage of going with a tour company comes with dealing with the Spanish fishery laws. These laws are enforced strictly and you need to get a licence to fish. Whilst I was there we were checked by two guys you seriously wouldn't want to argue with. In addition to that, there are issues with the use of boats. All boats need to be registered and to register them you are supposed to have relevant paperwork (like a car log book). As you can pretty much only get this paperwork by buying your boat in Spain, this is somewhat problematic. For me it's far easier to let the tour company do all of that for you and keep your holiday money in your pocket, rather than hand it over in fines.

On the tour back to Caspe from the airport I bent my guide Jamie Woods' ear relentlessly with questions about the zander fishing in particular, and the river in general. Jamie has spent a fair amount of time learning about the zander fishing from the locals, the visiting German anglers and others. In that time they had enjoyed some great sport, with multiple catches of zander – anything up to thirty fish in a day. That sounded like my kind of fishing, plenty of runs with a better-than-average chance of a biggie, and boy do they grow in the Ebro. The Spanish record currently stands around the 18kg mark; that's around 40lb. A zander of that size is just mind-blowing to an English angler, and the possibility of putting hooks in such a beast is what got me there in the first place, and will be one of the reasons for me to keep on going back.

However, such a fish is, of course, the fish of a lifetime. What about the reality? Again that

My first Ebro zander, caught on the first day on a whole bleak.

was a pleasant surprise, as not only is the scenery stunning, but the fishing ain't half bad either. Due to a number of factors, we decided to tackle the Ebro English-style, dead baiting from the bank. One of the main factors was to see how English-style angling worked as it's not the way that many foreign anglers fish and it's a style that many visiting British anglers would be familiar with.

Another experiment that we were going to undertake was to test out the zander's reaction to different hooklength materials. Many people have commented how foreign anglers tend to go ultra-light with their equipment, light braid and fluorocarbon hooklengths being the norm. Jamie had been tutored first-hand by the German anglers into fishing this way, using very long hooklengths and large single hooks threaded through the bait, and this was the way in which Jamie began fishing. On the other hand, I decided to start off with a standard treble rig on wire on one rod, the other rod being fished on a catfish Pro catlink Kevlar hooklength to a smaller single hook (size 2).

On the first day we fished from a nice, gravely beach that dropped away very quickly into water of around thirty feet, with just a few big boulders at the water's edge. Very quickly we were into fish, or at least we were getting runs – and this was where the first step of the learning ladder began. The zander were amazingly sensitive to resistance; just the lifting of a swinger was enough to get them to drop the bait. Both Jamie and I tried every way we knew to lessen this resistance, but we were absolutely plagued by dropped runs. This was to become a recurring theme through-

out the rest of the trip, these zander being so, so finicky and very delicate feeders. This really caused us to get our thinking caps on in the restaurant that night. Over a bottle of the local Rioja we talked over how we could change the ratio of runs into fish.

Eventually we got it spot on, and the results were far more runs converted into fish on the bank. The main change was to go down to the size 2 hooks and either catlink or fluorocarbon hooklengths, but instead of the whole bleak that we were using, we changed it to halved baits. The heads were hooked straight through both lips, whilst the tails were mounted by placing the hook through the tail, then turning it around on

Guide Jamie Woods hand-landing a zander.

itself and hooking again, so the hook sat close to the middle of the bait, the eye being threaded into the tail root. This hooking method proved to be the most successful of them all and, somewhat surprisingly, seemed to be the preferred part as far as the zander were concerned. This really upped our catch rate, and we started to regularly bank fish, albeit mainly in the 4 to 5lb range.

We persevered with wading through the schoolies, the theory being that, very much like in England, there will be bigger fish amongst, or close to, the packs of smaller fish. In the quest for this bigger fish we kept mobile, trying different areas, before ending up for the final day in the spot I liked the most of any that we fished. This swim was a large, rocky peninsula sticking out into the river, with another smaller tributary entering the Ebro to my right, and a large, shallow bay beyond that. The water here dropped away very quickly over a rocky ledge, and was crystal

Unhooking an Ebro zander, made easy by the use of single hooks.

In January the fog was ever present in the mornings.

clear. Water clarity seemed to be far less of a factor on the Ebro than it would be back at home, largely, I feel, because of the general depth of the water. In fact, in Jamie's conversations with the German zander anglers they had definitely expressed a preference for the clear water.

We were once again quickly into zander, schoolies again being in abundance, but an added problem soon arose that we hadn't accounted for – the rocks here were horrendous. This caused us numerous problems, the first being that the hook points were very easily blunted, or turned over. The next problem was that unless the rigs and fish were brought up quickly, the links tended to catch in the rocks. I went through three packets of Fox booms before switching over to the leger links that the foreign anglers use. These consist of a weight mounted within a plastic tube and a free-running ring at the top. These were far less inclined to snag up and stopped that problem; however, the rocks were to get the last laugh.

As we again went through the smaller zander Jamie finally lifted into the type of fish that we were looking for. The rod arched over and gave the tell-tale thumps of a big zander trying to shake loose the thin sliver of metal now embedded in its lip. The rod stayed arched over and thumping as I made my way along the rocks with the net, but just as it seemed that the zander was going to appear from the depths disaster struck, as the zander made the sanctuary of the rocks, and with one final shake of its head shredded the 15lb mainline. To say that the air turned blue would be something of an understatement.

On the last day we caught loads of fish after changing rigs and bait size.

Half baits resulted in more hook ups.

So the trip ended without the big zander that we had desperately tried for, but yet despite this apparent failure I definitely viewed the trip as a success. The fishing was great, with plenty of action to always keep you doing something. On top of that it was extremely challenging, touch legering at times to avoid resistance, hitting bites as fast as possible to avoid the dreaded resistance. Certainly the English style has its place in the Ebro angler's armoury. However, the really exciting part for me is to go back again and try the different methods from boat and bank and to add to the knowledge of the species.

Without question the Ebro is one of the most stunning places to fish, in terms of both the fish and the wildlife. Kites and vultures regularly soar overhead, whilst various wild animals some-

times appear for a drink, including Lynx and wild boar. Added to all that is the fact that with the Catfish Capers style and times of fishing you get the chance for a good night's sleep or to visit the local restaurants, which are excellent.

As a first-time visitor to the Ebro, and Spain, I was absolutely enthralled with the place. I shall certainly be going back there on a regular basis, for both the zander and to try and break my catfish duck. I also fancy going after a 30lb common carp, otherwise known as Ebro cat fodder! I can see the Ebro becoming popular with English anglers in the near future, only for zander rather than the catfish for which the river is justifiably famous. With the ultimate size being far beyond England's record it will surely become a must on the zander angler's hit-list.

13 DREAM ZANDER: SOME ACCOUNTS OF THE CAPTURE OF THE FISH OF A LIFETIME

Leigh McDonough, Dave Marrs, Ian Weatherall and Mark Barrett

My 17lb 12oz Zander from the River Severn

Leigh McDonough

I was pleased to be asked to write the story of my fish of a lifetime. I was a 14-year-old schoolboy at the time (I am 21 at the time of writing). Although I was only young I had been predator fishing for roughly three years and had already caught pike to 22lb 12oz.

The day in question was a Tuesday, and I was on a half-term break from school. My dad had decided to take the day off work because the well-known pike fisherman Dave Horton was coming to do a slide show for our local PAC region (Pike Anglers' Club) and we had arranged to spend the day fishing with him and another friend, Steve Bown, on the River Severn. As usual, we arrived before first light on a mild February morning. The boat was quickly set up, the rods and equipment loaded and we were in position on our first swim just as the sun was rising on a misty River Severn. The river was in perfect condition – rare to find it so.

We planned to employ our usual method of fishing – namely live baits, one rod each on a paternoster setup and one rod each to trot baits down the swim. The trotted baits were to be fished under our home-made balsa wood floats, made for this particular style of fishing, which were baited with a 6in roach, lip-hooked on a size six treble. We preferred to fish lip-hooked small baits because they were livelier with a minimum hook attachment. We gently lowered them off the back of the boat.

The paternoster rods were cast out to either side of the boat. These were a bigger live bait, with a double hook set up. We cast out the paternoster rods one either side of the boat. I then baited the trotting rod with a small roach, and trotted the bait down the swim to a hump feature on the riverbed.

With no take forthcoming I placed the rod in the rod rest to set about my breakfast. A couple of minutes later – halfway through my sandwich – the float disappeared and the bait runner came to life. I dropped the sandwich, picked up the rod and bent into the fish. Initially it didn't fight that much – it must have swum towards me. However, on nearing the boat the fish turned just under the surface, leaving a large swirl, and made off towards the middle of the river. I then realized that it was a decent fish and had a fair amount of power and weight to it.

After a minute or two of playing the fish, it surfaced behind the boat. Up until this point I didn't realize I was playing a zander, but now it was in sight I was looking at the biggest zander I had ever seen, whilst thinking, 'It's on the end of my line.' I tried to stay calm but shouted to dad to get the net quickly. 'I've got a flipping huge zander,' I shouted, or words to that effect.

Dad netted it relatively easily and also unhooked it there in the water. He collapsed the net and got me to hold the net and fish in the water, whilst he wound in the other rods and made for the bank.

On reaching the bank dad tied up the boat and made ready with the unhooking mat with the scales, weigh-sling and camera. I, for my part, was still in a bit of a daze, as you will see from the photos. We weighed the zander thinking it would probably be a mid-double, but were astounded when the needle pulled it round to a whopping 17lb 12oz. This was incredible as the record zander at the time was 18lb 10oz, also caught from the Severn by Ray Armstrong.

Leigh McDonough's 17lb 12oz monster; just look at the depth of this leviathan.

We were now in a dilemma. We were expecting our friends Dave and Steve to arrive, but they were nowhere to be seen. We decided that it was such an incredible fish that it should be witnessed properly. So, to retain the fish safely, we sacked it up and sat watching it carefully.

Fortunately we didn't have to wait long before Dave and Steve appeared, coming up the river in Steve's boat. We called them over to the bank. On arriving, Steve said, 'What's in the sack?' I replied, 'It's a seventeen-pounder.' He looked a bit bemused – obviously thinking it was a pike. I continued, 'but it's a zander.' He was now more shocked than bemused and made for the bank to tie his boat up. Both Dave and Steve got their cameras out and we then repeated the weighing process for them, with two different sets of Avon scales, and they then took some quick photos. The fish was then returned to the water – with its huge head held upstream – until it powered off out of my hands. We gathered ourselves and

continued fishing, catching several pike to mid-doubles and some much smaller zander. It was a great day. The following weekend we were back on the river and I must have been on a bit of a roll as I had a 21lb 8oz pike. I will probably never see or catch a zander that big again, but it will be worth trying.

Playing a Hunch

Dave Marrs

From the moment that I decided to write this book there were a few stories of captures that I desperately wanted to include. Dave's was one of those at the top of the list. I am sure there will be some who think a 13lb 11oz zander is not exactly earth-shattering news, but I beg to differ. Zander of that size are hard to come by now and will, I feel, always be so. However, the reason why this story just had to be in the book was more because of the instinct and dedication involved in its capture. After all, how many of us would travel a long distance from home for a short session to a swim they had never fished before, all due to a pure hunch?

This story more than any other sums up what it is about zander that grips us all, gets us out on the banks in some pretty horrendous condition, and keeps pulling us back despite the highs and lows that zander fishing throws us. It's Dave's story, though, so I will let him tell it.

When Mark asked me for the story of my personal best for his book I have to say that, initially, I was a little reticent. At 13lbs 11oz it was indeed a great fish; however, sadly it is no longer a weight that will set the angling world alight. Yet the circumstances behind its capture are as interesting as the fish itself, and as a fairly run of the mill angler I found myself thinking, 'Why not?'

The story starts on a Saturday night spent fishing the Twenty Foot Drain near Whittlesey, back in October 2003. I had enjoyed a session fishing for zander, catching a nice fish of 7lb 8oz. Although it could be said that this was a pretty average fish for the Twenty Foot Drain, this in fact

is a compliment. Sure, you don't tend to get too many large bags of zander, but those you do catch are normally of a decent average size.

Sadly, that night I had only the one run and the one zander which was, as mentioned before, a reasonably normal occurrence on the drain. Looking back, it was one of the quietest nights I'd had that autumn. The season had really been a bit of a blinder, already having provided me with a couple of doubles. I'd recently landed a fine fish of 10lb 10oz from the Ely Ouse and had been managing a few fish from both the Ouse and the Twenty Foot. Once night was over and the darkness gave way to the light, I noticed some small fish topping towards the far bank, and that was it. Out with the waggler rod for some hardcore bait catching, I was soon enjoying myself catching a few nice roach and rudd, all destined for the bait bucket.

Once daytime was fully established, the famous Fen wind started to pick up and the bait catching grew a little quieter. I looked at my watch and it was about 9.30am. Time to go, I decided, so I started to stow my equipment away and get ready to depart. My good friend and fellow zander hunter Nick Clare lives pretty much exactly half-

Dave Marrs with a Twenty Foot double.

A Fen sunset – the 'witching hour' commences.

way between my spot on the Twenty Foot and my home, so as I set off I wondered if he'd appreciate a visit. There was no need to worry on that score as within ten minutes or so both Nick and I were chewing the fat, slurping coffee and chomping on a nice bacon sandwich each.

Nick is as passionate about zander as any angler I've ever met, and quite naturally we both talked endlessly about zander. Which venue, in our opinion, would produce the goods? What size zander would our favourite venues offer? These were just a couple of the topics we discussed. All too soon it was time to head home and I made my excuses and began the drive home.

As soon as I left Nick's I was consumed with a strange feeling I've felt only a very few times previously, a feeling that had me positively itching to get back on the bank. Unfortunately I had a big day at work ahead of me the next day and, as keen as I am, there was no way I could afford to fish the rest of Sunday and the night too. I've done it before, but regrettably I had too much equipment to sort out for work and, besides, fishing is supposed to be fun! Still, there was no getting away from the fact that the feeling was growing inside.

I arrived home and squared my equipment away in the garage. I sorted my pump out to ensure my lives remained fresh, and re-packed my rods and tackle in order that it would be an easy task to pack my car for the next trip out. After that I decided to go for a couple of beers in my local. As I walked the two miles or so to the pub, I was mentally mulling over my thoughts, and the feeling I was experiencing was getting stronger and stronger. That evening, safely back in my house instead of getting on the couch with another beer and the remote control, I actually made up a few traces, further fine-tuning my equipment.

I was up at about 7am and soon on my way in to work. I had decided to fish a longish evening session that night after work, my normal après work sessions lasting from about 6.30pm until about 11pm or so. All day I tried to focus on work but my whole being was simply screaming to be in the Fens and, more importantly, in a swim on the Great Ouse that I'd only ever looked at a couple of times over the eight years or so I'd been fishing the river. Work was difficult, as everything that could go wrong, went wrong. I'd hoped to work

*Dave Marrs with an
Ouse nine-pounder.*

One that always made me feel like it would pay off.

through lunch and leave a little earlier, perhaps 4pm or so. Nightmare of nightmares, instead I managed to get out of work an hour later than normal, at 6pm, and didn't get back to my house until a quarter past. I was just opening my fridge door and taking out a nice, cool Tennants when my mind exploded and I came back to life thinking, 'What on earth am I doing? Let's go!'

I arrived at the swim at 7.50pm after a typically poor eighty-mile drive. No sooner had I switched off the engine than my phone went and I had to politely tell my brother I'd phone him the next night. A strapping ex-boxing champ with a millimetre fuse, I hoped he hadn't taken offence. Then, just as I landed my bait bucket and equipment on the top of the flood bank, the bailiff, John, turned up. I very meekly explained that due to a long drive I only had a couple of hours to fish. John seemed to understand, took my money and left. I hoped I hadn't come across in too churlish a manner.

I looked at the area and decided on a two-rod, paternostered live bait approach. I also made the decision that I would fish for four hours, then pack up on the stroke of midnight. The rods were baited with good solid roach of about 3oz apiece. One was dropped into 14ft of water under the rod tip, the other being cast to the middle of the river. There was no quick run for this session but, as the time quickly passed, at no time did I feel that something fantastic wasn't going to happen. In fact, as the hours seemed to zip past, I couldn't help feeling that something great was going to occur. The feeling I'd been experiencing for the best part of two days was in fact a classic hunch, an emotion I'd felt a couple of times before, yet one that always made me feel like it would pay off.

It was soon 11.45pm, and as I sat on top of the flood bank surveying my surroundings, the nearby pub and the ripples crossing the water as the breeze grew stronger, one of my ghetto-blasters emitted its rather obnoxious tone. I slid down the bank and struck into a good fish, soon under control. I netted a rather large pike that I thought would go 20lbs+. Upon weighing, it went 18lb 6oz, a very nice fish indeed, yet

it wasn't the result I thought I was going to get. I returned the fish and sat back on the bank to enjoy my last ten minutes or so. The breeze had got up and the drizzle became more earnest in its attempts to soak me, but luckily my Sundridge Minus 10 suit was foiling the misty dampness. At the stroke of midnight I decided enough was enough, it was time to slide down the bank and retrieve my rods.

As I approached the inside line rod another odious tone belted out, the drop off hitting the bank stick with a resounding thump as it fell. I picked up the rod and struck. I thought, 'This is it,' as I connected with another fish. The rod buckled into a satisfying bend as the zander hugged the bottom with no small amount of vigour. I thought it must be a good size. After what seemed like only a couple of minutes all went slack and a nice zander popped belly-up on the top. I thought, 'That'll be another double, then' when all of a sudden I realized that it was still about three rod lengths out and in the middle of the river. My legs went to jelly as I carefully played the by now well-beaten zander to the net. The relief I felt as it was drawn into the big nets mesh was simply immeasurable.

Upon lifting the net from the water I realized that this fish was enormous. The hooks popped out with a deft flick of the forceps, much to my relief. I'd only seen a head the size of this zander on one other, some seven years earlier. That one was 14lbs and to this day is the biggest I've ever seen in the flesh. Upon first weighing of this fish, the scales flickered around the 15lbs mark. Once fully composed, having stopped flapping and got a grip, I registered a weight of 13lbs 11oz, beating my personal best by 1lb 8oz.

Unfortunately the batteries in my new digital camera died, and instead of replacing them I took the pictures on my rather aged 35mm camera, which I hadn't used for a year or two and hence they turned out a little poorer than perhaps they should have. My soul was chewed to pieces as Mark gave me a rifting the next day for not having given him a shout to take the pictures. 'You fool, Dave, I'd have loved to see that fish and take the pictures. You should have given me a call!' Back

Dave Marrs with his big zander.

at the riverbank, I put the fish back in after only a couple of minutes and after a little coaxing she swam back to her watery haunt with a powerful flick of her tail. I was now exhausted. Emotions running high, I quickly packed up and headed for home. It was an extremely happy journey and I sang my head off all the way home.

Looking back on this capture, there were a few factors that fell into place. I'd squared my equipment away and everything was in great shape, my bait was as fresh and as good as bait is ever going to be. I'd put in a lot of effort – how many other guys would travel a 160-mile round-trip after a hard day's work to fish a four-hour session in the Fens for zander? The conditions were perfect and indeed that night turned very cold and was the first frost of the year, always a night I've rated very highly. Most importantly, I'd listened to my feelings. My hunch had told me to fish a remote swim I'd never fished before; I followed my hunch, went straight ahead and I fished it. I have to say that I awoke the next morning with a very big grin on my face. Work was a joy as I happily volunteered to make the tea, much to the amazement of my colleagues. As a fairly average angler, ten years to the month after I'd landed my first zander I'd finally smashed the 13lb barrier!

A Pair of Sweet 16s

Ian Weatherall

With the arrival of my driving licence came the possibility of targeting the fish that had fuelled most of my angling thoughts over the previous couple of years – a fish that lived in far-away Fenland waters, which had captured my imagination with its strange and beautiful appearance.

The early years of my zander apprenticeship saw me introducing myself to famous waters such as the Sixteen Foot, Cut Off Channel, River Delph and Great Ouse. Fish were often encountered once I'd managed to get my head around the venues and rigs deployed, but despite the regularity of captures it was becoming obvious that the larger fish just weren't coming out, at least not to my rods. I think the best zander I'd had on the unhooking mat prior to 1990 was around 7½lb from the Ouse.

On the odd occasion I met and chatted with other zander anglers on the banks, another water I'd yet to fish kept cropping up in conversation, a drain that was beginning to get the reputation for larger than average zander – the Middle Level Main Drain.

The Middle Level Main Drain – a water that was capable of providing captures to blow you away.

My first few exploratory trips to the Middle Level were what I would term gruelling. The drain is famous for its horribly steep and wind-swept banks, at times with very strong flows and more often than not producing completely blank sessions, added to which it gets covered in a thick surface weed most summers. All in all, it's an awkward drain to fish. Trips with very limited success became the norm and any runs would be classed as a triumph. Yet the water still fuelled my anticipation when an alarm sounded; it is one of those venues when the next fish could either be a schoolie zander or the next British record.

With despondency creeping in I was encouraged by the results of other anglers, in particular Ralph Hughes and a guy who I befriended called Mark Jones of Telford. It was Mark who managed to capture a 16lb zander and a 20lb pike in the same session during 1991 or 1992, I remember. I recall him telling me how he chose to fish the stretch because of a nearby pub, a result for sure, but his decision could hardly be described

as watercraft. I kept plugging away during this period, becoming more and more desperate in my quest for the first fish over double figures. Things finally began falling into place, and the following couple of tales detail my Middle Level highlights at a time when the drain rocketed into zander angling folklore. Over ten years later, thinking back, this period was the most magical episode of my angling life to date. It was a real learning curve, on a water that was either capable of providing captures to blow you away, or where you could fish hard week after week for very little return.

The Tip-Off

It was the August Bank Holiday weekend, 1993, and I had planned a three-night weekend trip to the Middle Level. I was unsure which area to settle in for the first night. Should I go back to a spot that produced a couple of fish to 9lbs the weekend previous, or go to a new spot on the map that I had a hunch for? Pastures new won the toss and I settled in for the night about a hundred yards upstream from one of the many bridges to cross the Level.

I soon cast four rods around the drain from my chosen pitch, with both lives and deads on to hopefully cover all options. Dusk soon approached as I settled on the bedchair, hopeful that this night would be the one. As the last rays of light sank in the west over the flat land, one of the alarms sounded to announce the arrival of a low double-figured pike. Before dawn a small zander also visited the bank, but when the morning sun rose the realization of another poor night began to sink in.

I was an hour or so away from packing the equipment up and moving when I noticed a vehicle approaching from the opposite side of the bridge. The van stopped and the driver got out. As he approached me I didn't recognize him. After a good chat, he introduced himself as Dave Gaunt. A nice bloke, for sure, who I think took pity on a poor northerner when I explained about my lack of doubles so far. He explained to me how he and a friend had been targeting a stretch downstream of the bridge over the last few weeks, and how it was producing doubles on each occasion they had fished it.

Information like that certainly got my attention. However, the downside of this hotspot was that it was a good mile from the bridge, and once there the fishing was very hard due to the sheer sided banks. In fact it was mentioned how Dave and his pal were using a ladder to get from the top of the flood bank to the water's edge some 10ft below. Dave said that I should try that area the next night, which was very nice of him, so with a daytime trip to Downham Market for provisions an excited angler made his way to the spot around 3pm later the same day.

The banks amazed me; I could see the logic behind the ladder technique now. I set up the best I could in the sunshine and settled down to await events. Sitting in my chair on top of the flood bank in the late summer sunshine, I knew

Ian Weatherall with an Ouse double.

things were going to happen. The first bobbin dropped off around an hour after setting up. With line racing off the open spool I wound down and hit into what I hoped would be a zander. Something had taken the small roach dead bait, but the resistance on the rod suggested it was also small. When a 2lb eel surfaced in a tangled ball, I muttered some derogatory comments under my breath and hoped I wouldn't be troubled with eels all night. When eels are moving on the Fens, any fish bait, be it alive or dead, on the bottom or mid-surface is a meal for them.

The next run, about half an hour later on the same rod, was very similar to the first. I remember feeling sure when I struck that it was going to be another eel. However, the rod kicked back on the strike and a very dogged fish allowed me to pump it back towards my bank. With two or three hours of daylight left, my thoughts were that it must be a pike – surely the zander aren't feeding yet. My surprise and relief when a big, spiky zander broke the surface were immense. All the hours chasing a double were surely going to pay off as the fish slid into the landing net. On the scales she weighed 10lb 2oz, and at that moment there was no happier an angler in the whole of Fenland.

Dave, his wife and his friend then turned up and set up about two hundred yards to my right. I reeled in and wandered down to his swim, as I was busting to tell him about my double. While I was visiting his pitch one of his rods was off and a nice 16lb pike was landed. I left Dave just before dusk to get everything sorted for the night-time zander bonanza to come.

The next couple of hours into dark proved to be slow. A couple of beers were enjoyed before the next run came along at about 10pm. I'd cast a small roach livey on a paternoster across the drain to land in the deep far bank margin, and the bobbin dropped like a stone as a fish came back across the water towards me. On the strike it felt heavy, just plodding around with the occasional head-shake. Once under the rod tip the fight got better, the fish taking line off me as it ran along the marginal shelf whilst staying very deep. I put the torch on to see big boils on the surface. Surely it must be a pike, I thought. Then I caught a glimpse of a huge zander twisting and boiling just under the surface. Don't come off now, please. Out with the landing net and in she went, first time. Talk about relief. The next problem was going to be getting myself and the fish up

Completely shell-shocked by the whole event. Ian Weatherall's 16lb 9oz zander known as Alex.

the vertical bank to the unhooking mat. Once the climb and unhooking were accomplished, I placed her in a net, unsure of her weight but realizing she was huge.

A quick run down the bank spluttering nonsense to Dave soon saw all them of them return to my swim to weigh and photograph the beast. Just as we placed the fish into the weigh sling, one of my other rods sounded, so I left the biggie in Dave's capable hands whilst I dealt with the other run. Another good fight followed, and unbelievably another big zander surfaced, although not as big as the one on top of the flood bank. I left the last fish in the landing net with Dave's friend whilst I went to have the photos taken with the big one. Dave had recorded a weight of 16lb 9oz and a length of 36in. It was absolute mayhem, leaving me completely shell-shocked by the whole mind-blowing event.

Photos taken, big, cheesy grin, and the fish was safely returned before starting the whole procedure again with the fish in the landing net. This one pulled the needle round to 11lb 1oz. Six hours earlier I hadn't seen a double-figure zander, yet I'd just landed three of them on the bounce. It can be a funny old game this fishing lark. One minute you can be a hopeful dreamer, and the next minute all your dreams and ambitions are realized.

After things had settled somewhat and Dave and party had retired back to their swims, I retreated under the brolly to dream the night away. As I remember, rightly or wrongly I even brought the rods in early as my head just wasn't up to the job of carrying on.

Despite my elation, I recall at the time feeling a bit uneasy about Dave telling me of his hotspot. I'm sure he would have been feeling the same – we were all blown away by the events. I needn't have worried, as over the next couple of months he had one or two of his own special moments along that stretch of water. At the time, however, I realized I would have to be very cagey regarding details of the capture, it of course being Dave's find, and such was the degree of cloak-and-dagger goings on regarding big zander captures at the time. Even to the point where, when I packed

up and reached the bridge to cross the drain the next morning, I bumped into fellow zander anglers Chris Peck, John Cranswick and Phil Coupland. There I was, bursting to tell the world of my good luck, and when they enquired as to how I'd got on, I had to reply, 'A couple of schoolies, mate.'

The 16lb 9oz fish proved to be the ninth biggest ever recorded at that time. A very proud moment, which I thought at the time I would never come near to again.

My Own Find
It was August Bank Holiday weekend again, but two years had passed. I travelled to the Fens hoping for a session like the one two years previously. On this occasion I was joined by my friend Paul Snowdon for a three-night trip exploring different sections of the Middle Level Main Drain.

Between my capture of the 16lb 9oz zander in 1993 and this trip in 1995, it had come to light that we were all fishing for two very large zander amongst other lesser, but still very big, zander. As mentioned above, Dave Gaunt had been plundering the drain's big fish. The zed I captured had been named by the regulars as 'Alex', with the other biggie gaining the tag of 'Non-Swimmer' because of her fondness for a particular stretch of water – in fact the same stretch of water from which I had previously captured Alex. I think both fish had been captured at around 17 or 18lb a few times by now, and from memory it was Non-Swimmer that generally came out a little heavier than Alex.

Paul and I set up about a hundred yards apart from each other, in the cool and windy conditions that we found ourselves in. I'd managed to make two clearings in the heavily overgrown banks just large enough to accept two rods in each spot, and so we settled in for the forthcoming night with a very limited supply of baits.

I recall always retiring to the sleeping bag full of hope and optimism whilst fishing the Middle Level, usually only to wake in the early morning light with hopes dashed, as the realization of another blank session dawned on me. The first morning of this trip fitted the description well;

at 5am I woke and began to contemplate, over a steaming hot coffee, a move to a different area. Not a single blip came from the alarms during the dark hours, so the surprise of an alarm sounding its wake-up call a little after 5am made me spill the coffee in a scrambled attempt to get to the rod. The zander had picked up a dead roach and was running parallel to the far bank at quite a speed. With Paul still fast asleep it was left to me to net the fish, which I thought initially to be double figures. It fell 6oz short of reaching the magical weight but was still a very useful fish to catch. So with photos taken, after shouting Paul to get up, we discussed our plans for the next night.

Whilst we desperately needed to stock up on live baits, I felt that we should spend another night in these two swims. Paul wasn't so sure because of the lack of activity from his swim, but once convinced we set about the task of filling the bait buckets. With me on the pole and Paul on the quiver tip, we fished in our respective swims the best part of four hours that morning. It soon became apparent we weren't sat on a shoal of silverfish, and with only a couple of tiny perch in the bucket I thought I would try around the bridge, upstream of our position. The many bridges along the drain often hold quite a few roach tight to the bridge features so off I went with pole, bucket and bait in hand. When I arrived at the bridge, I found that all the best pegs had been taken by a group of Yorkshire pole anglers. After a quick chat with one of them, it became apparent they were slaying the roach and hybrids using hemp and tares with the average size of fish caught being around 12oz. So I dropped in below them and fished maggots, the only bait I had with me. My pole limitations really came to the fore that morning, and two hours later all I had added to the bucket was a single roach about 3in long.

Another chat with the angler upstream of me resulted in him offering me a few fish out of his keepnet, and as soon as the offer left his lips I had the bucket lid off in anticipation. He had around fifteen pounds of fish in the net but struggled to find much around the 4 to 6 ounce range we were after. I think he let me take a dozen or so roach

and hybrids ranging from 6 to 12oz, which really helped us out. After thanking him profusely I packed up the pole equipment and rushed back to our main swims. Paul thought the larger of the baits were too big so he helped himself to the smaller roach, leaving me the bigger hybrids amongst the small perch and roach.

The day drifted quietly into evening, a meal was prepared and a vast quantity of tea was drunk. As we prepared our rods for the night I remember putting a small perch live bait to the far bank margin where the nine-pounder came from the previous night. A roach live bait went on a straight lead to the middle of the drain, and two of the larger baits went on paternosters in the near margin. Despite fishing 3oz leads on the paternosters to hold the larger baits in place, they still kept giving false runs. I put up with this until around 9pm, but didn't relish the idea of getting up every half an hour through the night to re-set the alarms. The larger of the two hybrids was causing the most problems so the decision was taken to fish this as a dead bait, reducing the amount of lead required but still fished about two feet off the bottom on the paternoster. With the rig lobbed rather than cast over the reeds in the margin, I retired up the flood bank into the sleeping bag.

Around 11pm a high-pitched drop off sounded – the large dead hybrid rod was away. Realizing it was a big bait I left the run as long as I dare before pulling into whatever had taken the bait. The rod arched over for a brief second before snapping back as the fish spat the hybrid out. When the bait was retrieved it was stabbed up as though it was a zander that had dropped it, and a good one at that given the width of the bite marks. A quick check for tangles on the paternoster tail and I sent the same large hybrid back out over the reeds, bite marks and all. As I knelt by the rod taking up slack in the line and clipping up the drop off alarm, the line was sharply tugged out of my fingers. It always amazes when this happens; surely the commotion of the cast would spook the fish. From the bait hitting the water to the time it was taken must have been about ten seconds. It was on it like a shot.

Absolutely euphoric, with a new personal best of 16lb 13oz.

Again I left the run to develop a short while. In fact it ran to my right under another rod that was luckily cast to the far bank out of harm's way. On the strike it took maximum side strain to gain line and pump the fish back under the far bank rod into safety. I remember knowing instantly this was a big fish, but I still hadn't seen it. Could it be one of those nocturnal pike that come out from time to time? As the fish came to the surface it boiled in the torchlight and revealed itself as a zander. She hit the net the first time of asking after a typically dogged fight under the rod tip, and the guessing game began. She was obviously very large, being incredibly stocky across the back with a defined hump on her shoulders. The tape showed her to be 33½in long, some 3in shorter than Alex. Into the zeroed sling she went, and the scales showed 16lb 13oz. I was euphoric at the realization that I had achieved a new personal best. She was placed in a large, spare landing net fixed to the bank and resting nicely in the deep margin water. I recall waking Paul to tell him my news. Despite being only a hundred yards away his swim was still very quiet.

We did the photos as soon as the light was strong enough in the morning, the fish holding her dorsal fin up proudly for the camera and snapping her jaw with a loud, audible crack. At that moment I pitied the poor silverfish population of the Middle Level. With a nocturnal beast like this on the prowl they certainly have a stressful existence. She went back very strongly that morning with a kick of her tail, sending a refreshing spray of water into my face.

I was later informed that the fish was in fact Non-Swimmer, ironically captured a couple of miles away from the section of drain from which she gained her name. I consider myself unbelievably fortunate to have experienced both of the famous Middle Level zander of that period on the bank, even though on both of my captures they weighed slightly less than they had for others.

For the final night of our trip, and because Paul had yet to catch, we agreed to move to another water not far away. I can't recall if Paul managed to save a blank on this second venue, but my fishing diary tells me I was lucky enough to land a couple of fish weighing 9lb and 10lb 14oz on this our final night. It was certainly one of those sessions that doesn't come along too often, when all you do turns to gold.

Over ten years have now passed since these captures and time has moved on. I still try now and then, and generally the fishing is still as hard as it was back then. The Middle Level Commissioners have removed a vast amount of the bushes and fauna along the steep banks, making the place seem even more featureless now than it was ten years ago. One question remains for me now, as it did back then, 'What chance a twenty pound zander from the Middle Level?'

Chasing Rainbows: A Magic 15lb Zander

Mark Barrett

Big fish of any species are hard to come by, predominantly because of their rarity. After all, not every fish is going to make it through to come close to its optimum size. Predation, death by natural causes or any other number of contributing factors take their toll on the population. Therefore by setting out to catch the biggest specimens of any species the angler has to be prepared to experience failure for the greater part, only rarely punctuated by those occasions when all of the pieces of the jigsaw fall into place. The stories in this chapter are typical of those all-too-brief moments of elation as their dreams have become, momentarily, a reality. This is my story of the moment that everything finally came right.

From the moment I started out as a zander angler the magic target had always been a 15lb + zander. Such a beast has always been to zander anglers the pot of gold at the end of the rainbow. Unfortunately for me, my rainbow-chasing had always seen the end just out of reach, and whilst the hunt was always enjoyable, it had become somewhat of an obsession to catch that magical 'fifteen'. I had come close of course on more than

one occasion. I had witnessed a 15lb 5oz zander from the Middle Level caught by my friend Glenn, I had even caught fish up to a little over 14lb. A massive zander by any standard, but it still didn't have the kudos that that phrase 'fifteen' conjured up in fellow zander anglers. Added to this quest was the fact that writing this book was looming on the horizon, and I so wanted to have my own massive zander to document. The obsession was burning brightly, but I was determined to quench it once and for all.

Christmas 2006 was just a matter of days away. The weather had been extremely wet over the course of the autumn. The rivers and drains had been out of their banks on more than one occasion already, but the weather had become more settled, though cold and foggy with it.

I grabbed my equipment and stowed it away in my Vitara to do a short evening session two Sundays before the Christmas festivities were due to

Continues on page 140

The scene on the Sunday evening.

Myths and Monsters

In common with all other fish species, the tales of uncaught or secretly caught monsters are legion. Tales of monsters that exceed the current or past record fish are pretty much as common as zander anglers themselves. But what is the reality or likelihood of there being truth behind the mystery?

The Relief Channel Pair

Two of the most controversial mythical monsters were reported as being set up by an Essex taxidermist, Albie Hall. These fish were both reported as coming from the Relief Channel in the 1980s. However, the method of capture has never really been explained. The official line was that the captors were given special permission to night fish the Channel, and that these fish were caught then, on rod and line. However, many people are actually of the opinion that if these fish were caught from the Channel at that point in time, the most likely way that they were caught was by 'dead lining'. This is effectively using a set line baited and then tied to the bank and left, usually for a night or two, to be retrieved when a fish has swallowed the bait.

This sort of behaviour has been practised for many years in the Fens (and probably other areas of the UK), and is on the increase with the influx of foreign land workers. The problem with this method is that not only is it highly illegal, but it is also pretty certain to result in a dead fish. The reality is that fish caught in this way are destined for the pot anyway, and in ancient times it was a way of life in the Fens. But the fact remains that it is against current fishery law, and this is often given as to being the real reason as to why these fish were never reported.

Whatever the reason for the non-reporting of these fish, there is some tangible evidence of their existence in that they were set up. A weight has never been officially reported for the bigger of the two, nor has the set up fish ever been seen in public, but the second fish appeared in July 2007 in a photograph in the *Angler's Mail*. This fish was reported as weighing 23lb, which was way in excess of the record at the time (18lb 8ozs) and even a good bit in front of the record at the time of writing of 21lb 4ozs. It's because of this vast differential that personally I find the stories hard to believe.

In most of the record fish where exhaustive lists are compiled there are usually several other specimens that are within 10 per cent of the current record. At the time of their capture, those zander would have been over 25 per cent bigger. That is quite some jump to take into account.

No doubts about this monster zander of 14lb 11oz for Glenn Gillett.

However, there is one way in which the attributed weights could have been possible, and this would also account for the fact that the fish were never reported to the press. It is possible that the fish were caught whilst heavy with spawn, meaning that they would have almost certainly have been caught out of season. In such a situation the possibility of such a fish becomes far more likely. The Relief Channel did produce a zander weighing 18lb 8oz in a netting survey carried out by the then National Rivers Authority (now the Environment Agency). This fish was well-documented and photographs have appeared in the press of this fish being held by Paul Wilkanowski of the NRA. Taking that as an example of the type of weights that the fish could achieve in the Channel at the time, a fish with a good meal inside it could just stretch to that kind of weight.

The reality is that only a very few people know the truth of the captures, both in method and true weights, and unfortunately they are not telling, so in these instances the fish will always be shrouded in mystery and controversy.

Netting Survey Monsters
Another rumour that has always done the rounds is that there have been very large zander caught in the netting surveys carried out by

The Relief Channel, home to two unverified mythical fish.

the authorities, be it BW or the EA. However, members of the EA's staff concerned with fisheries work deny such fish have been caught. The biggest fish caught still remains that 18lb 8oz fish from the Relief Channel. However, in the future there is a likelihood that the amount of actual nettings will decrease as a lot of fisheries work is done by acoustics. Netting will always happen, to determine what is showing on the acoustic survey, but in these days of maximum conservation actual handling will almost certainly be reduced.

James Benfield's Record Zander
One fish that is not an enigma is the record fish caught by James Benfield from the River Severn in 2007. News of this fish began to filter out towards the end of June 2007, and it really staggered the zander fishing world, as, of course, the UK's first-ever 20lb zander was always going to. However, what really threw the zander anglers was the method of capture. The fish was caught on a halibut pellet intended for bream! To many zander fanatics, and I would class myself amongst their numbers, the method of capture took some of the gloss off the capture. However, none of that is the captor's fault and at the end of the day the record list is of course only a note as to the biggest fish caught on rod or line. What they decided to choose on that day is immaterial.

Night falls and the monsters come out to play...

Continued from page 137
start. My venue was to be the Great Ouse along Ten Mile Bank. I had chosen this stretch as it had produced my fourteen-pounder a few years earlier, but more importantly it had a track record of producing some great catches of very big zander if, as I suspected, the bream had moved into the area as relief from the floodwater that had recently arrived.

Upon reaching my chosen stretch I pulled the jeep up onto the top of the bank, an added bonus to this stretch, and took a look at the water conditions. The river was showing signs of the heavy rainfall of the autumn, in that it was carrying a brown tinge of colour, but it was certainly decreasing, and though the current was certainly up enough to make fishing the far bank awkward, it wasn't raging through as can often be the case.

Enthused by what I had seen I set about putting the rods together, and it wasn't too long before four rods were perched on their rests waiting for a zander to announce its arrival through a screaming Delkim. However, it was not a zander that got there first, as shortly after starting a jack pike was lifted clear of the water. I replaced the rod and bait and, as I sat watching the rods with the day slowly slipping away, I became aware of a large shoal of bream rolling about a hundred

yards further upstream. This sight really fired me up, as I knew from previous experience that this would mean that the big old zander wouldn't be too far away. That evening passed by fairly quietly, with just an 8lb zander to show, before I packed away at 10pm.

Despite the modest returns of this Sunday evening, I knew that I had to get back here at the first opportunity that I had. Unfortunately I couldn't get back the next night as I had a prior football commitment, but Tuesday night saw the jeep once again parked up by the river. The weather had remained settled, but had got a good degree colder, and foggier. In fact the day had been so foggy that the overnight frost had not lifted from the grass, and to be honest my optimism wasn't very high. I doubt, if I had been aiming to go anywhere else, that I would have bothered, but nothing ventured, as the saying goes.

It had not even got dark when I had my first run, though contact was only fleeting with whatever had tried to make a meal of my live roach. Still, it was an encouraging sign that anything was willing to feed in such bitterly cold conditions. After the early action the night went reasonably quiet, only being punctuated by the occasional bleep caused by drifting weed. I had arranged with a friend of mine to drop off his copy of a new

The Sunday evening eight-pounder.

carp book, which I had picked up for him at the weekend, at 8pm, and the clock was slowly going round to that mark as I sat in the jeep listening to a football match on the radio.

Just as I was beginning to think that time was up, and I was to return fishless, my mobile rang. It was the friend I was going to see, telling me that he would be out for a bit longer than he had first expected to be. That was indeed a result, as it would provide me an extra hour in which to try to end my blank. I very much doubt that the clock had gone on five minutes more when my furthest rod, which was cast down the near shelf, signalled a series of bleeps. I was quickly on the rod and felt down through it to the bait, whereupon I could feel a slight tugging upon the line. I swept the rod back and felt the satisfying thump of a fish on the end.

Whatever it was that I had become attached to wasn't enamoured by the fact and strove to stay as close to the bottom as it could – a sure sign of a big zander. Eventually I managed to get the fish up close to the surface, where it began the usual zander ritual of thrashing its head from side to side. I had lost a good fish from the same swim a few months earlier at this point, and was praying under my breath that this one would stay attached, as by now I could see that it was indeed a big fish. Fortunately I managed on this occasion to bring the fish over the net. Here events took something of a comic turn, as the net had frozen solid from where it had been in contact with the frosty bank. Usually just dipping the net into the water is enough to defrost it. However, this time the water itself was bitterly cold and for an agonizing few seconds the zander was balanced upon what looked like a giant tennis racket.

Again my luck held, and with a bit of jiggling of the net on my part the mesh eventually fanned out and was lifted around the zander, which was illuminated in the beam of my head torch. I lifted the fish up onto the unhooking mat, and it was only then that the true size of the fish struck me, such was its depth and girth. In fact I am pretty sure that I have caught far longer fish than this one that weighed around the 12lb bracket, but

The scene that greeted me, though Christmassy, wasn't very zander friendly.

The pot of gold and an ambition achieved – 15lb ½oz.

none have had the dimensions of this one, more reminiscent of carp than zander. Up on the scales the needle hovered between 15lb and 15lb 1oz, so I just split the difference. Finally, the magic fifteen mark had been breached, albeit with very little to spare.

I rested the fish up in the net in the margin so that I could get a photographer down to help – there was no way that I wanted to make a mess of these pictures. My friend Glenn came over and took some great shots of the fish.

There seemed little point in carrying on anymore, after all it would have been greedy to have expected a similar prize to the one already bestowed upon me. I packed my equipment away into the jeep and left to drop off my friend's book – the book that inadvertently caught me my dream zander. I had finally got my pot of gold.

14 ZANDER NOW AND IN THE FUTURE

The zander angler has, arguably, never had it so good as they do today; certainly the travelling angler has far more options available to them than in years gone by. The spread of zander across England has seen them reach geographically as far north as the River Trent, though there have been zander (and may still be) in Tyram Hall in Doncaster. As this spread has happened, so has the popularity of zander increased, as this book stands testament to. Due in part to this rise in popularity, more and bigger specimens are being reported from some of the 'lesser' rivers such as the Thames. At the time of writing the Thames and the Trent have begun to produce fish over 13lb in weight. Rivers such as this will see their population increase and grow, and potentially within the next twenty years could be up there with the more established zander waters to produce the next record fish.

With luck this spread will see the zander become 'accepted' as a species within the UK. In the Fens where I live and fish they are already

The Old West, where I first cast a line for zander.

The author with an Ouse double, a river on the up for all species.

accepted. No longer do you see lines of match anglers throwing zander up the bank, though the threat to zander has metamorphosed into Eastern European anglers who are brought in to work on the local farms. Only the vigilance and determination of local anglers has kept this in check so far, but it is a situation that needs monitoring. To that end, in my local area fishing clubs and the EA have set up a river-watch scheme, which I am proud to say I am co-ordinating. However, because the Environment Agency still keeps zander on the alien species list, and as long as it does so, the zander is not afforded the same level of protection that our other coarse species enjoy. The irony of this shouldn't be lost on any angler who lives in the Fens in particular, as it was the EA in a previous incarnation as the Great Ouse River Authority that stocked the zander in the first place.

Of course zander anglers of the past did not help the image of zander when they illegally introduced them to river systems in the Midlands. Here the situation is not quite as rosy. There certainly are some very keen and talented anglers within that region, as will have been seen elsewhere in this book, and the potential of the Avon

and Severn is mind-blowing. Yet the Midlands remains as one of the hotbeds of match angling, in particular canal fishing, and here they are far from accepted. For many years British Waterways had a 'kill all zander' rule, and some anglers act as though they still do.

Thankfully the electro-fishing of zander has stopped, a result that the Zander Anglers' Club and Pike Anglers' Club had been campaigning for, for many years. I could never understand BW's stance on this, as the history of the Fen cull should have shown them that this course of action not only cannot work, as the ultimate aim is elimination, but on the Fens resulted in a boom in small zander that caused more problems.

To be honest the only course of action is to wait for nature to take its course, as unpalatable as it may be to some. This will take over ten years, as self-predation and age are all major contributing factors to the 'levelling off' of the zander population. One could argue that in the Fens it took thirty years from their original introduction to reach a natural level. Certainly the waters in the Fens are now alive with prey fish species. However, this doesn't take into account the effect that the cull had in actually maintaining the zander at an unnatural bio-diversity. After all, the population consisted of high numbers of very small zander, a situation that is no longer evident. My feeling is that a period of twenty years would see a stable zander to prey fish biomass.

Zanders' Impact on other Predators

One population that definitely will take a downturn after the introduction of zander is the other predators in the water. Nature maintains a prey-to-predator balance, and as much as the zander affect the prey fish population by tipping the balance in favour of the predators, they also affect the predator population when taking their position as nature redresses the balance. This can affect the established predator population in varying ways. On some waters the zander will find the environment very much to their liking and may become the dominant predator. A good example of this would be the Great Ouse Relief Channel, site of the first zander introduction. Until zander were introduced, the Relief Channel was well known as a prolific big pike water. There were other influencing factors but the part that zander played in the demise of the Channel as a pike fishery can't be overlooked. These days the zander is without question the dominant predator to the extent that after many years of fishing the Relief Channel I am yet to catch a pike from it.

In stark contrast is the River Lark, which joins directly to the Ouse near Queen Adelaide, just outside Ely. The confluence of these two rivers is a known and popular zander spot, yet despite fishing the Lark for many years for pike and perch I am yet to land a zander from it. Yet one would consider it as ideal for zander. The food population is on the whole quite small, the water holds a nice amount of colour, and it's shallow, so fairly warm, yet as a zander fishery it's hopeless. Here the pike and perch have seen to it that a population has never really got a foothold, and it is not alone. The Little Ouse, though better than the Lark, has never really been colonized, as have other rivers, like the Wissey.

I do wonder if perhaps perch have a part to play in all of this. If you look at the time that the zander was introduced, during the 1960s, the perch population was at an all-time low after the perch epidemic. As the zander spread so the perch have also recovered and it doesn't seem a great coincidence to me that the waters where zander have struggled to gain a foothold are good specimen perch waters. Maybe part of the reason is that the competition for very small prey fish

Ian Welch with his personal best, caught on a night fishing with the author.

A stunning Ouse zander of 12lb 6oz.

is too great for the zander. This is no more than speculation on my part, but it does have a ring of truth to it. Whatever the reason, zander do not pillage every fishery that they enter. In fact on some waters the introduction of zander will see an increase in the ultimate size of the pike, if not their overall numbers, as pike most certainly see zander as just another meal.

Where Will It End?

So where will the spread of zander end? It's a difficult question to answer, as some would say that eventually the zander will spread throughout England and maybe even across the borders into Scotland and Wales. This may of course come to pass, but I for one hope that it does not. I know that that may sound like a selfish statement from someone who lives in the heart of zander country, but the reality is that for the zander to spread in that manner it will need man's assistance. That assistance will do far more damage than just in the water into which they are introduced, particularly in the eyes of the general angling public and the powers that be.

The species will never be accepted whilst illegal introductions are taking place, as they impact upon some anglers' fishing and they do no one

any favours in the long run. Furthermore, it is hard to say what the anglers who introduce these fish are expecting. After all, zander are a fairly slow-growing species, even in favourable conditions, and if a fish was stocked at 4lb it could take another five or six years to reach double figures, if (and it's a big if) that water is capable of producing such fish. If it is not, all the angler has done is to further sully the name of zander and those who pursue them, for absolutely no benefit.

Admittedly, without illegal introductions there would be no fish in the Trent, Avon or Severn (the Thames may have actually got there via an accidental introduction via the Lea and in turn Grafham Water), but whilst those fish have proved an interesting diversion to anglers in those areas, the fact is that the scare stories have continued because of it. If we are serious about the protection of the species as a whole then those anglers involved need to consider these issues seriously. Looking at the bigger picture, introducing zander is just not a good idea. It may mean that some anglers need to travel to catch zander, but hasn't that always been the way? In my own fishing, if I want to catch barbel, I have to travel around fifty miles to catch reasonable specimens, and if we are talking about the likes of grayling or salmon the distance involved would be in the hundreds of miles.

Grafham Water – a water of the future?

Maximum Potential

Moving away from the spread of zander, what about potential growth rates in the zander themselves?

We all know that on the continent zander grow far bigger than we have seen so far in England. However, the really big zander seem to come from the colder climate countries such as Sweden, Russia, etc. This could largely be down to fry recruitment, in that the colder water offers less chance of successful spawning and fry recruitment. To be honest I don't know enough about the countries involved to pass judgement.

Looking at France, even there zander have attained greater sizes than in England. However, fishing in France is somewhat different to here in that most predators are taken for the pot and there is nowhere near the concentration of anglers that there are in England, particularly predator specialists. So logically the zander has a much better chance of reaching its optimum weight as they lead a relatively stress-free life.

The same cannot, of course, be said for fish in England. Though there are certainly fewer zander anglers than, say, carp or even pike anglers, most of the 'more likely' waters do see a large number of zander anglers at certain times of the year. However, there are still waters that remain relatively untapped, even in the Fens, which sees more zander anglers than any other area. The best example of all is the Relief Channel. Even if it were to be fished hard, with limited access and its sheer size the Relief Channel could always throw up a surprise. If the evidence of recent seasons is anything to go by, then hardly anyone is actually fishing the place. I find it amazing that a water with a track record for producing big zander and with increasing stocks of prey fish sees such little attention from committed zander anglers.

I would certainly put the Relief Channel on my list of potential record waters, alongside the other known big fish water of the Fens, the Middle Level Main Drain. The Main Drain, of course, has a track record second to none for pro-

Alan Ward with a massive Grafham zander of 17lb.

ducing outsize zander, and to this day it continues to do so. However, the going here is hard and the stocks are low, always good conditions for the zander to grow very big. It will always throw up a big fish from time to time, as was seen by Mark Knowles' 18lb fish of 2002.

So where else in the Fens could produce a huge zander? The Cut Off Channel has in the past thrown up the odd big zander and there is always the chance that it could do so again, but the recent form of the water has not been great, and I think the chances of it threatening the record in the near future are slim. Another contender could be the Great Ouse. The Ouse and its tributaries make up a vast system, and it has thrown up some nice zander. I have had them from the river myself to 15lb, and I know of other fish to over 15lb from both the main river and the Old West, its old course.

There have been other fish reported from the

Ouse, to over 17lb, but the fish that I have seen have been nowhere close to the claimed weights. I know that photographs can be misleading, but I have asked several other anglers whose opinion I respect, and the responses are unsuitable for publication. The best example of this is one fish reported as being over 16lb, which, upon further inspection, turned out to be the same fish I caught at 14lb 2oz. As the fish was reported in the same month as mine, it had either gone on a massive binge, or a crash diet, depending upon which side of my capture it had been caught!

Whether these fish are entered at higher weights by design or by not believing the scales is not for me to comment upon. I know that I have looked at a few zander and thought that they would be close to the magic double figures, but that turned out to be very short, especially at night in the torchlight. However, a fish weighs what it weighs and it greatly annoys me and others that the record lists

The author's brother Paul with a 13lb 4oz fish from the Ouse.

are being polluted by these fictional fish. I predict that as the fish gets into the media more frequently these fakes will fade away, as editors and writers become more familiar with what is and is not a big zander. Things are slowly starting to improve, and of course with the Severn throwing up a new record in 2007 of over 21lb the bar has been set just that bit higher.

Figments of the imagination aside, the chances of the Ouse throwing up a big zander are very good but, and this is a u-turn from statements I have made in the past and one that I am sure will come back to haunt me, I don't think that the Ouse will threaten the record. My reasoning for this is simple – there are just too many zander on the water. In my guiding guise I nearly always fish the Ouse as there are greater numbers of fish in there than any other water, with perhaps the exception of the Old West. Too many zander equals too much competition for food and

though the stock levels of prey fish are currently high, the Ouse seems to increase its population, rather than increase its optimum size. Furthermore, the zander on the Ouse just seem to level out around the 15lb mark, even though they have the body length to go on. To provide an example, in 2000 I caught a fish (which I have seen caught a few times after) at 12lb 6oz from the Ouse, which was 33in long. I have not seen that fish weigh more than 13lb 3oz, though it is always in very good condition and was still at the same length four years later.

My fishing friend Glenn Gillett caught a 15lb 1oz zander from the Middle Level in 2003; it was also 33in long. That's nearly 3lb difference on its lowest weight and 2lb on the Ouse fish's maximum weight. I think that they are good reasons for this, the main one being the size of prey encountered by both fish. The stocks on the Ouse are predominantly in the 1 to 4oz range on aver-

Glenn Gillett with a big Middle Level zander. The Level will produce monster zander again some day.

age, the fish in the 4 to 10oz range being far fewer, in part I think because more match and pleasure fishing takes place on the Ouse than the Level, and small fish are retained in keepnets, which does very small fish no good at all. On the Level, however, the average stamp of fish caught whilst catching bait is 4oz and above, to a size that is not really feasible for zander angling. Therefore once the zander have reached a reasonable size there are plenty of bigger prey fish available.

Having said all of that, there is always a chance with the Great Ouse that a monster could emerge from the pack that completely rewrites the expectations for that river. After all, the 15lb fish that I caught from the Ouse was actually quite short, being less than 33in long, but had a huge girth. If this fish was young enough it could conceivably push on past the 16 or even 17lb mark, but I remain to be convinced that the Ouse will ever be a water that will threaten the record, particularly in light of its history of never having produced a reported 18lb+ zander.

It may be a sad fact for the Fen zander fanatic that the record is going to move away from the Fens forever. With it standing now at over 21lb, there's still a long way for the Fens to go to catch up. In reality if the close season is ever lifted on the drains, then there may then be the opportunity, but at what price? I believe the close season should remain as it is on our rivers and drains, even if that means that ultimately I may never catch a 20lb zander in England. I can live with that, especially if it means that the fragile ecosystems that are our rivers and drains retain a degree of protection.

We may have to continue to look to the Midlands for the biggest zander in England, a situation that my good friend John Cahill will relish as he refers to Midlands zander as 'proper zander' after I used the same phrase to describe Fen zander in a talk I gave to his PAC region. Certainly the last five years (2002–07) have seen a real dearth of top-end zander, by which I mean fish in excess of 16lb. In fact in the winter in which I caught my biggest zander, that of 2006/07, my catch was the third biggest reported for the year.

I certainly would not have expected that the Fens would fail to produce a really big zander, but in reality there have been only a few reported since 2002. If you contrast that with the record of the Severn and the Avon in the same time span, then the two Midland rivers win hands down. The real acid test for those two waters, though, will be in the years to come. As zander are now gaining a reputation in the area their population is likely to increase as fewer are destroyed. It is a strange dichotomy that, for the really big fish to come through, a small population is better than

One of my favourite zander pictures, of my friend Russ Brennan with an eleven pound Middle Level zander.

A recent Middle Level twelve-pounder.

A zander caught while preparing a feature for Total Coarse Fishing *magazine, something I'd like to do more of in future.*

large numbers of zander, and to that extent culling, as abhorrent as it is to zander anglers, may in part be contributing to the very large zander that the area is producing.

Whether the UK will ever regularly produce twenty-pounders is open to conjecture. There certainly seems to be something that inhibits coarse fish from reaching their ultimate weight. If you compare our record fish lists to those on the continent they do not hold up well in general, so it stands to reason that we are unlikely to reach the same sizes of zander as on the continent. However, there are waters that could yet see zander pushing on beyond the limits

that we have seen so far. To my mind the waters that we have that come closest to those that produce huge zander abroad are the reservoirs that hold numbers of zander, namely Grafham and Rutland Waters. In 2007 a 14lb zander was caught from Grafham Reservoir on a fly, so the fish are creeping up in weight. If you could only fish for them in the same ways that we can elsewhere, then I am sure that one of these reservoirs could really shock the angling world. However, to be able to do so, a major shift would be needed in the attitude of Anglian Water to coarse anglers.

A POLITICAL ANIMAL

Non-native Fish

When you look at the spread of zander from a purely evolutionary viewpoint, their population of the Fens has been nothing short of remarkable. After all, with just ninety-seven fish being introduced into the Channel it is something of a miracle that any survived at all, let alone that they went on to populate the entire Fen watercourse. That they achieved all of this tells us a lot about the adaptability of the zander as a species. This ability to adapt and to overcome also shows us the inherent problems that there can be in introducing any new species to an ecology.

In this day and age the introduction of a non-native species to the rivers and drains of the UK would not even move beyond the ideas stage. DEFRA and other relevant governing bodies would not countenance this for a minute. In fact, the whole subject of the introduction of non-native species is very much to the fore. The UK is currently undergoing a purge of illegally stocked fisheries, or stockings without the relevant paperwork. The angling press has regularly carried news reports of another fishery that has been ordered to remove or to destroy their stocks of predominantly catfish and sturgeon. Anglers have quite rightly been up in arms about this state of affairs; all an angler wants to do is to catch fish, and though some may stop to consider the wider environment and issues surrounding fishing, painfully few actually do.

A fly-caught Grafham zander is brought towards the boat.

Paul Newman with a stunning Grafham zander of 17lb 2oz.

The truth of the matter is that by all definitions the catfish should, according to DEFRA's own guidelines, now be classified as a native species as it has resided in the UK for over a century. That it is still not considered a native fish is, in my opinion, due primarily to the paranoia surrounding all predatory fish, as was seen with the spread of the zander.

The experience of continental countries also has an influence. In Spain, for example, the River Ebro was illegally stocked with Wels catfish, and the effect that they have had there has been quite devastating. However, there are reasons why the cats in Spain did so well, and these are not the same as in the UK, climate being the main one. Higher mean water temperatures mean that the cats in Spain get a better chance to breed. In the UK, though some breeding does take place, the recruitment of fry into adult fish is very low, and so populations stay low. Zander, on the other hand, can survive and breed in water temperatures far lower, and thus they recruit well and populations thrive. When you bear in mind that catfish have been present in the Great Ouse for decades, yet the number of anglers that have caught one is minute, you can see that there is still no viable cat population.

The one spanner that the authorities will always throw into the works against this argument is that of climate change. Whilst most would agree that the climate is getting warmer, the UK still does not achieve the mean temperature of water of continental rivers, and I personally doubt we ever will.

But how does this attitude to alien fish species affect zander anglers? The main impact is the stringent controls that are placed upon live baiting.

The Future of Live Baiting

It is already illegal to use live fish other than in the waterway from which they are caught, and in time many feel that the use of live fish as bait will cease completely, as it already has done in Scotland and Ireland. It is hard to argue against this becoming the reality, as there are many within angling who feel that by sacrificing live baiting it will somehow appease those who wish to see the end of angling per se. I believe they are wrong; as far as the anti-fishing lobby is concerned, fishing by any means is abhorrent. They do not care where and how we place hooks into fish, they don't want us to do it in any way, shape or form. If anglers sacrifice live baiting it will only appear as though we are somehow nervous about the whole debate.

If there is one thing that history has taught us, it is that appeasement is never a viable negotiating tool. Personally I feel that when the time comes and live baiting is in the cross hairs, the reasoning behind banning it will not be made on moralistic grounds. My view is that the ammunition of choice will be the spread of disease and the introduction of alien species, indeed I hope that this is the case as I firmly believe that there is a foothold there by which to fight the ban.

Whenever the notion of the spread of disease through the use of live baits is mentioned, there is one glaring hole in the science of the matter – there is not one documented case in the UK in which the introduction of disease to a waterway has been directly attributed to the use of live baits. Looking at the subject objectively I would have to concede that there is a possibility, albeit it a very small one, of this happening.

A particularly worrying aspect is the popularity in the last few years amongst pike anglers of using carp as live bait. Here I believe we are treading on thin ice. Carp are one of the biggest carriers of diseases in the fish population, and even more seriously they happen to carry two particularly devastating diseases – KHV (koi herpes virus) and SVC (spring viramia of carp). Both of these diseases can be absolutely catastrophic to a water's carp population if introduced. This has

been seen time and time again where new stockings have been made into fisheries, followed by an almost total wipeout of the existing population. Add to all of this the fact that these diseases are very difficult to detect, certainly impossible to the untrained, and they become something of a potential ticking bomb. Should a pike angler inadvertently introduce one of these diseases to a high-profile carp water then a movement to ban the use of live bait completely will be triggered. With the way that the angling industry is built upon carp angling, this would be a movement that I feel would be completely unstoppable.

It is not all doom and gloom, though, and whilst we still have the opportunity to use live bait I shall certainly continue to do so. After all, the fish that we are choosing to catch has evolved and adapted to feed on live fish as its primary source of prey. It may well be that in years to come we will have to adapt ourselves and become more proficient in the use of lures and dead baits to continue to catch, but at the moment, given the choice, my first line of attack would always be a live bait.

I am often asked about this when I am doing talks and slideshows around the country for branches of the PAC. The main reason I now turn to live bait as a first choice is simply because when I tried it my results were so much better than before. In that first year I caught nine doubles in one season, a tally that still remains my best for a single year, and was way ahead of any single year prior to that point. That's not to say that deadbait fishing plays no part in my zandering anymore; it still does, only now I prefer to use it in specific circumstances where I think it may have the edge, such as coloured water conditions.

Zander Conservation

The conservation of zander is another important issue that we will need to address in future. Whilst most anglers will already know something about handling and returning zander properly, there are certain areas in which we are still lacking in knowledge of how best to do this. The most glaringly obvious is the issue of catching zander from really deep water. In the past this was never really an issue, as the rivers and drains it has been confined to in the UK are rarely more than twenty feet deep at best. However, with the advent of boat fishing for zander on waters such as Rutland and Grafham, there are many zander anglers expressing real concerns over zander's long-term future in these waters.

The concern centres mainly around the fact that a lot of these zander are being caught in depths of over fifty feet, and when brought up to the boat they are suffering what can best be described as something similar to the 'bends'. What this means in practice is that the zander are suffering from a distended swim bladder, which has over-inflated and causes the zander's stomach to appear through its mouth. This is a pretty common occurrence in sea angling where fish are caught over very deep water, but the difference there is that most of the fish are destined to be killed anyway. Obviously that's not the intention, for the greater part, of the anglers fishing on Grafham and Rutland. The cause of this problem is in the zander itself, as they are not able to regulate the pressure in their swim bladder, like many other fish. The only real way to negate this influence is to get the zander quickly back down to the depth from which it was caught.

On the continent, where zander are caught regularly at great depth, the anglers there often employ what has become known as the 'torpedo technique'. Now this technique will look pretty abhorrent to most UK anglers at it pretty much flies in the face of all that we usually practise in terms of handling, as you literally propel the fish into the water from a good height head-first. It's not quite as daft as it first sounds, as this action creates a large amount of pressure on the swim bladder and stomach, and forces the fish downwards quickly.

Having little experience of this myself, although I can see that it might help, I have huge reservations about it from a practical point of view. First, whilst that may put pressure on the swim bladder, this may not be of an equal amount to that produced at depth, and additionally the

pressure would only be at that level for a short period of time after the initial impact. As the zander slowed down, so the pressure would drop. Second, this method relies upon the zander swimming straight down to the bottom. From my experience of zander that are in any kind of distress from capture, this is pretty much the last thing that they do; instead they tend to come to the top of the water and just waddle about. I am not saying that the torpedo method cannot work – I am sure that there would not be so many anglers willing to use it if that were the case – but those same anglers are not going to be around for very long and it is quite possible that these fish are turning up dead at a later date.

Another method that I have heard of, and one that I believe may have some mileage in it, is to employ a spare rod with a large weight on. The zander is gently hooked up onto this via a light line and lowered back straight away to the depths, whereupon as it recovers it breaks the lighter line when it has regained its strength. This seems to me a better method, as it certainly will get the fish back to the depths quickly, though obviously there are limitations to it and it is quite fiddly to get right, the worst case scenario being that the fish comes up from depth on more than one occasion. However, I shall try this method myself in the coming months on Grafham and Rutland.

It goes without question that there are fish dying on these waters. Whether Anglian Water will come out directly and say so though remains to be seen; after all, the the pike/zander fishing on the water is a good revenue earner for them in a historically quiet trout fishing period. However, I know of several big fish that have been washed up at Grafham Water, where currently most zander fishing is taking place. The biggest of these is a 17lb fish that was given to a taxidermist to be set up. Whatever way you look at it, though the fish will not go to waste, it is a tragedy that fish like these are not surviving the experience of being caught.

So what can be done about this? I guess, in the short term, very little other than to look to the continent as much as possible for a guide. On mainland Europe zander are often caught at great depths and zander fishing ultimately has stood

If you look carefully you can see the swim bladder inflation problems on this zander of 15lb 10oz caught by Colin Brett.

the test of time, so they are either very lucky in having waters that are capable of sustaining the losses, or they are more knowledgeable in how to return fish to depth.

I would tend to favour the latter as it should also be remembered that on the continent there are far more instances of fish being taken for eating than in the UK. The French and Germans in particular take large numbers of fish from rivers such as the Ebro, and pike in Ireland. I have myself seen German and French anglers on the continent take away large numbers of fish for the pot. The French love most fish. I can well remember on a carp-angling trip to France watching a local angler emptying his keepnet full of roach and rudd into a washing-up bowl to be taken home to make bouillabaisse (fish soup). The number of pike that Germans in particular took back

home from Ireland became such a problem that the Irish fisheries boards put a limit upon the amount of pike flesh that any one angler could take per day. At the time of writing there are plans afoot to increase this limit drastically, as it is felt that it is dissuading continental anglers from visiting Ireland. In my opinion restricting the limit would be preferable, but pike are still considered non-native to Ireland so it is not altogether surprising.

Developments at Grafham and Rutland

Despite the problems that there certainly are in fishing these waters, the fact remains that the fishing on Grafham and Rutland opens up a new world to the zander angler, and the prospects

You can clearly see the size of jigs used to catch this Rutland zander.

for the water are quite mouth-watering. In the 2007/08 season Grafham produced bigger zander than it had done at any point in the past. Rumours abound of two fish in excess of 23lb being caught from there. So far there has been no confirmation of either of these fish, and that makes me wonder if either of them are genuine, particularly as they were supposedly caught by accident by trout anglers.

However, zander have been caught on Grafham to over 18lb in 2007. Add to that a number of back-up fish caught between 12 and 17lb and that equates to a pretty healthy zander population, even if a number of fish have died. There is every chance that the zander here will go on to break the British record, possibly by some margin. When you consider that the zander have not been in Grafham very long, to have attained the weights and growth that these fish have in such a comparatively short space of time certainly augers well for the future. If those rumoured fish in excess of 23lb are not currently true, I can certainly see a time when Grafham does go on to produce fish in the same sort of class. In fact the success of the zander population may go a long way to an-

swering the question posed by a number of pike anglers on the reservoir – namely, where have all the pike gone?

It certainly seems that the zander have found Grafham to their liking, and as such they have pushed the pike into second place. Pike anglers will be bemoaning this fact, but there are plenty of trout waters that are open to pike anglers, whereas this is the first zander trout water. Actually, the enigma here is that the trout in all probability are quite immaterial to the zander, as most Grafham trout have been stocked at a size that should make them too big for zander to catch (2lb+), to avoid excess cormorant predation.

The fact is that Grafham has a massive population of coarse fish that thrive in glorious isolation other than the occasional accidental capture by fly anglers. You only have to look in the boat yard during the times when the reservoir is open to predator fishing. The entire boat yard is usually covered in masses of fry, which must number in the millions, such is the area of water that they cover. This gives the juvenile zander plenty of chance to grow on quickly to the stage where they are quite able to tackle bigger prey, of which again there are plenty. Denis Moules, who wrote the sea bait chapter in this book, was fortunate enough to catch a 12lb 6oz zander from Grafham in the autumn of 2007; it then suffered the swim bladder problem I mentioned earlier, but in doing so it coughed up its last meal, a fish too well digested to identify, but weighing at least 8oz. As a great supporter of the big bait theory for larger zander, I personally felt a certain amount of smugness at being proved correct, but more to the point it shows that there are plenty of fish there of the best size for maximum growth. Remembering in earlier chapters the relevance of prey size to growth rates, it is easy to see that in Grafham, a water that is only open one month a year, we have an amazingly exciting potential for zandering in the years to come.

What, then, of Rutland Water, which holds a younger population of zander? I envisage that the zander in Rutland will also grow to a good size. We will have to wait and see whether they will achieve weights similar to those of the zander in Grafham. At the moment they are relatively modest in comparison to Grafham, but it is worthwhile remembering that the zander have only been in Rutland for half as long as they have in Grafham and in ten years' time they could well achieve similar weights.

Vertical Jigging

Both Grafham and Rutland give the zander angler the chance to fish in a manner that is still relatively underused in the UK, using jigs, and in particular vertical jigs. Vertical jigging is probably one of the commonest tactics on the continent, and can certainly be a devastating way of fishing for zander. On the continent vertical jigging takes place with gear that most anglers in the UK would baulk at. Very light rods, braid down to 4lb breaking strain and fluorocarbon hook lengths are the order of the day, and yet still these continental anglers land some very large zander and pike on this tackle.

I personally cannot see this way of fishing taking off, due to the emphasis placed on conserva-

tion and preservation in the UK. In part this is born of necessity, as there are more anglers and fewer waters than in continental Europe. In addition, I remain to be convinced that the reasoning behind the use of the ultra-light gear stands up to scrutiny. Continental anglers insist that the tackle is necessary, particularly the light braid, in order to have maximum control and feel of the jigs at great depth. Though when we are talking in such small dimensions between, say, 8lb and 15lb braid, it is hard to see that it would make as much of a difference as is claimed. Perhaps it is the case that, as this is the method that nearly everyone is using, the fish are just getting wise to this and a complete change of tactics might be just as successful.

In reality, UK anglers would be ill-advised to use tackle such as this, as it could well see them ejected from many UK waters. Seemingly, though, UK zander are not as picky as those abroad anyway, as already some very large hits of zander are being caught on jigs and flies from the two reservoirs. With the current restrictions on angling methods to lures and sea dead bait only, it looks like UK anglers will have to become proficient in the use of jigs if they want to tame some of the beasts from the deep!

In Conclusion

As zander anglers we will always be involved directly or indirectly in fishing politics, in that the fish that we choose to pursue is vilified and acclaimed in equal measure. It's a sad fact that some angling writers still choose to use zander as a benchmark against which to measure the ills that can be attributed to the introduction of 'alien' species. For that reason alone zander will probably remain in the news throughout my lifetime, almost certainly predominantly negatively. As a keen zander angler and an angling writer I will always emphasize the positives of zander angling, such as the additional revenue that can be brought in for clubs. I fear, though, that much like a tidal water zander, we will always be swimming against the flow!

INDEX